DATE DUE			
JUL 13 '73			
OCT 21 2004			
GAYLORD			PRINTED IN U.S.A.

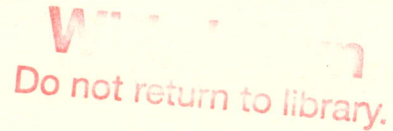

Do not return to library.

THE STUDY OF RELIGION on the CAMPUS OF TODAY

Selected Papers From the Stony Brook Conference on Religion as an Academic Discipline

Edited by
KARL D. HARTZELL
and
HARRISON SASSCER

Andrew S. Thomas Memorial Library
MORRIS HARVEY COLLEGE, CHARLESTON, W. VA.

ASSOCIATION OF AMERICAN COLLEGES
WASHINGTON, D. C.
1967
77116

377.1
H259s

FOREWORD

The Stony Brook Conference on the teaching of religion as an academic discipline was held in January 1966. It might reasonably be supposed, therefore, that a selection of papers from this conference would be somewhat out of date when published in 1967. Fortunately, the editors feel no need to apologize on this account, for there is ample evidence that the topics discussed at Stony Brook are as timely now as they were when the conference was held and that the papers delivered there provide thoughtful and relevant insights into these topics.

The response to the brochure "Religion as an Academic Discipline," issued by the Commission on Religion in Higher Education of the Association of American Colleges in December 1966, indicates that academic administrators and faculty members in many different types of institutions—church-related, independent, and public—are giving serious thought to the role of religion in the academic program. Thus, the issuance of these papers and the detailed summary of the vigorous discussion that they prompted at Stony Brook will, we hope, prompt similar vigorous discussions on many campuses. Indeed, perhaps administrators, teachers, and even students from campuses that are convenient to one another geographically will be motivated to hold "Stony Brook Conferences" of their own.

Some of the papers that are presented here were originally delivered from manuscript, but most of the participants in the conference spoke from notes while their remarks were being tape recorded. The discussions that followed each presentation were also tape recorded, and one of the editors (Karl Hartzell) assumed responsibility for listening to these and extracting from them the review of the discussion included in this volume.

The editors would like to acknowledge the invaluable assistance of Mrs. Julie Scheuermann of the staff of the State University of New York at Stony Brook, who transcribed the tapes upon which many of the papers included herein are based, and of Miss Laura Kent of Washington, D. C., who helped with the final editing of the manuscript.

We wish to express our appreciation also for the work of the program committee which, under the chairmanship of one of the editors (Dr. Hartzell), planned the program and invited the speakers. The other members of this committee were: Bishop John J. Dougherty of Seton Hall University, J. Alfred Martin, Jr., of Union Theological Seminary, James G. Murray of Adelphi University, John W. Pratt of State University of New York at Stony Brook, Harold Stahmer of

Barnard College, and R. B. Y. Scott of Princteon University. The amenities of meals and accommodations for the participants, along with other logistical details, were handled by a committee on arrangements drawn from the Stony Brook faculty and chaired by James A. Fowler, assistant dean of the College of Arts and Sciences. Other members of this committee were: Donald Goodman, Edward Malloy, John W. Pratt, and David Tilley. President John S. Toll, who served as a member of the committee ex officio, was host at a late evening reception and buffet for the participants following the close of the conference.

Finally, we are grateful to President Richard H. Sullivan and the Board of Directors of the Association of American Colleges for their interest in the success of the conference and for making possible the publication of these papers.

K. D. H.

H. S.
March 1967

Publishers' Acknowledgements

The passage from "Leda and the Swan" is reprinted with permission of The Macmillan Company from *The Collected Poems of William Butler Yeats*. Copyright 1928 by The Macmillan Company, renewed 1956 by Georgie Yeats. The passage from "A Dialogue of Self and Soul" is reprinted with permission of The Macmillan Company from *The Collected Poems of William Butler Yeats*. Copyright 1933 by The Macmillan Company, renewed 1961 by Bertha Georgie Yeats. Passages from *The Collected Poems of Edwin Muir, 1921-1951*, are quoted by permission of the Oxford University Press; the passage from "Prime" from *Selected Poetry of W. H. Auden*, is quoted by permission of Random House, Inc.

CONTENTS

Foreword iii

Publishers' Acknowledgements v

Background and Purpose of the Conference vii

Religion as an Academic Discipline:
   Characterization of the Phenomena To Be Studied 2

Comments on the Study of Religion 6

The Function of the Study of Religion 9

The Nature and Formulation of Academic Disciplines 16

The Scholarly Study of Religion in College and University 22

Reflections on Michaelsen's *Scholarly Study of Religion* 26

The Study of Religion: A Family of Academic Disciplines 33

"Objectivity" and the Study of Religion 38

Modern Poetry and Religion: A Deepening of Perception 42

Review of the Discussions 50

Appendix 75

INTRODUCTION

Background and Purpose of the Conference

The Association of American Colleges has from the beginning included among its members private and public institutions which have been concerned with, among other things, the place of religion in the intellectual life of colleges and universities. The continuing examination of this question is the principal assignment of the Commission on Religion in Higher Education, one of the five standing commissions of the Association. Within the past three years, the Association has sponsored several conferences or dialogues on phases of this subject. Experience with these conferences led the commission to conclude that there might be value in limiting the range of discussion to topics of more precise definition. The State University of New York at Stony Brook offered to serve as host to a conference that would provide institutions in the Long Island-Metropolitan New York area with an opportunity to consider the place of religion as an academic discipline in the college and university curriculum, its position among the humanities, and its relation to the rest of knowledge. This conference represented an effort to examine and clarify the principal issues that arise in connection with the teaching of religion on college and university campuses.

Underlying the planning of the conference was the commission's belief that students at the undergraduate level should at least have an opportunity to reflect on the great questions of our Western religious traditions—questions which they themselves, in the course of their personal development, ask—and to examine the impact which man's religious convictions, when translated into action, have had upon cultures in all ages and all parts of the world.

Attendance at the Stony Brook conference was by invitation and was limited to a maximum of 50 persons, one faculty member and one administrator from each of the 27 participating campuses. In the hope of insuring that a lively diversity of views was represented, the planners sought to include a wide range of institutions—public and private, large and small, Catholic, Jewish, Protestant and nonsectarian.

The purpose of the conference was to bring together a relatively small group of participants that they might, through informal discussion, explore such questions as what the nature and function of the study of religion as an academic discipline is; how the study of religion relates to other areas of academic inquiry in colleges and universities and to the renewed concern for the humanities evidenced by the establishment of the National Foundation on the Arts and Humanities; whether public and private institutions have differing responsibilities and opportunities in this field or whether an academically appropriate concern for the study of religion is the proper business of all institutions; and what means may be used to implement a viable program for the study of religion in colleges and universities. It was hoped that, by coming together in a kind of multiple dialogue, representatives of institutions in the New York area who were in positions of influence and responsibility would gain added understanding of the importance of the field of religion itself and would be encouraged to provide adequately for it as a discipline in their institutions.

The conference was organized into four sessions and a final roundtable. A bibliography of reading materials was collected and sent to each participant. Included were Robert Michaelsen's *Scholarly Study of Religion in College and University* (1964) and his *Study of Religion in American Universities: Ten Case Studies* (1965) (both published by the Society for Religion in Higher Education) and a report on a Conference on the Study of Religion in the State University, held October 23-25, 1964, at Indiana University. Additional recommended reading included the report of the Commission on the Humanities published in 1964 by the American Council of Learned Societies: two Supreme Court cases, *Abington Township* vs. *Schempp*, and *Murray* vs. *Curlett et al. School Commissioners of Baltimore*, 374 U. S. 203 (1963): and descriptions of the course offerings of such departments of religion as those at Barnard College, Princeton University, and Wesleyan University.

Religion as an Academic Discipline and its Subject Matter

Religion as an Academic Discipline: Characterization of the Phenomena To Be Studied

J. Alfred Martin, Jr.

It is entirely appropriate, I think, that we should begin our consideration of religion as an academic discipline in the college and university with a session devoted to characterizing the phenomena to be studied. If we are to have meaningful and productive discussion, we must at the outset establish the broad outlines of a frame of reference for that discussion, and we must generally delineate the structures and dimensions of human experience which come within the purview of the academic discipline called "religion." These preliminary steps are necessary because so much debate as to whether there is such a discipline and, if so, whether or how it should be pursued and taught in colleges and universities, has been vitiated by too narrow an understanding or by an insufficiently critical and informed understanding of what we are talking about when we speak of religion as a subject matter for appropriate academic inquiry. The disputants assume views based on various kinds of personal and social involvements in the religious traditions of their own culture or on the particular interests and methods of their academic field, thus distorting or prejudging the issue. Therefore, an initial sharing of views on what the appropriate subject matter of inquiry may be in the scholarly study of religion is imperative.

It is also felicitous, I believe, to cast our preliminary discussion of this matter in the framework of what the planning committee for this conference terms "characterization of the phenomena." This phrase is appropriately inclusive and flexible, and at the same time it suggests the necessity for careful and responsible descriptive work. Note that we do *not* begin with a *definition* of religion or with a detailed discussion of the problem of definition or with a search for definition. Essays in definition have, indeed, been a significant part of some kinds of study of religion—particularly of philosophical study, but also of historical, psychological, and sociological study. The task of definition should not be abandoned. But it is important that one know what he is and is not doing when he engages in that task, and it is important that he know the task is unending so long as

---

The author is Danforth professor of religion in higher education at Union Theological Seminary in New York.

critical, philosophical, or any other sort of inquiry into religion continues.

Actually, the concept "religion," and the view that it is something that can and should be defined, are central only to Western thought and, moreover, to Western thought of only the last two centuries or so. The whole enterprise of conceptualization and definition assumes certain interests and directions of inquiry. It assumes that, from the plethora of practices, institutions, and beliefs which we now, at least in the West, tend to encompass in the term "religion," we can abstract some common or normative essence; it assumes, further, that from this common or normative essence, we can deduce or develop further patterns of classification and methodology. Nineteenth-century thought especially abounded in essays in definition, and a careful inspection of most of these essays reveals the distinctive philosophical and social-scientific assumptions and convictions of the definers. Thus Schleiermacher could associate religion with the feeling of absolute dependence, beyond all partial dependences and concerns. And earlier, Kant could speak of religion as the recognition of duty as being divinely grounded or sanctioned. Still others could define religion in terms of its intellectual belief-structure—usually making a distinction between "natural" and "supernatural," or between world and man and God.

Mind you, I do not believe essays in definition are totally inappropriate or irrelevant to the study of religion. As a philosopher of religion, I am particularly fond of such essays—of the problems they entail and of their implications. I am saying only that we should know what we are about when we engage in this kind of inquiry; we should recognize that it is not the sole, or even the foundational, inquiry for the study about which we at this conference are concerned. Wilfred Cantwell Smith, the historian of religion who now directs the Harvard Center for the Study of World Religions, has reminded us in a thoughtful and provocative book, which has the intriguingly ambiguous title *The Meaning and End of Religion*, that few if any followers of those ways of life which we tend to call "religious" have thought of themselves as members or practitioners of a religion—at least not until recently, in some Western circles and societies. The relation of what some of us call "religion" to culture in all facets is extremely complex and various. But it can be said, Professor Smith points out, that objective and sensitive inquiry, academic and nonacademic, shows that there are *people*—in all of the variety and richness of individual humanity—who understand themselves in terms of *traditions;* and that these traditions entail and are expressed in practices and institutions ranging from tribal dance to plain chant, from kiva to temple and synagogue and cathedral. The practitioners of these traditions may be saddhus or shamans, priests, rabbis, or evangelistic preachers. These traditional institutions may, at one extreme, be virtually identical with general cultural institutions; at the other, they may be self-consciously opposed to them. But in all of these phenomena, suggests Professor Smith, there is some sense of, and some expression of relation to, "transcendence."

Now the term "transcendence" is itself vague and may even be contentious. Suffice it to say that, in all those traditions which encompass the phenomena we wish to characterize, some fundamental distinction is made between the ordinary and the extraordinary, or the natural and the supernatural, or the profane and the sacred, or the phenomenal and the noumenal, or the penultimate and the ultimate. The distinction is real, and it is important; indeed it is in a sense constitutive of the phenomena we wish to consider. But its specific intellectual and structural articulation varies from culture to culture and from tradition to tradition.

We should concern ourselves here not with debating the merits or demerits of specific philosophical, theological, or social-scientific renderings of religion or the religious. We should concern ourselves first with noting well the fact that there are phenomena—that there *is* that which *appears* in human experience—and that there are phenomena which are complexly and intriguingly distinctive from other phenomena and which bear complex and intriguing relations to them. Concretely, these phenomena are as varied as churches and orders, theologies and religious psychologies, solitary mystics and ecclesiastical bureaucracies, systems of ethics and foundations of values, manuals of devotion and commercial doggerel and purest poetry. In other words, religion—if we continue to use the term because we lack a better one or perhaps because it is impossible to find a better one, given our historical situation—religion is simply a *fact*. Religious institutions exist. Religious philosophies and theologies are entertained and believed in. Religious art is created; religious literature is written.

Our task, then, is first to note the fact that religion is a fact. And then we must ask what we should do about that fact if we are faithfully to discharge our responsibilities as institutions of higher education. We cannot and should not wait until we have formulated a mutually acceptable definition of religion, or arrived at a full and careful characterization of the phenomena involved, to raise that question. After all, we do not wait upon definitions of art or of history before engaging in the study of art or history and providing appropriate academic structures for such study. Let us simply note that there are scholars who are concerned about, and who devote their special critical attention to, religious thought, religious institutions, and religious practices. In the course of their inquiry, as in the course of many other inquiries, peculiar constellations of method and emphasis have emerged from the inquiry itself. The phenomena tend to set the scale. But the inquiry is open-ended: indeed, we would seem to be in the early stages of rapidly expanding insights into the complex character and relations of religious traditions. The problem of the methodologies and the styles entailed, given the broadly human character of the phenomena, makes a consideration of the study of religion as an academic discipline a microcosm of the macroscopic concerns that the higher learning has with all things human. And I think it can be said that what a college or university does about the academic study of religion is a good indication of what it conceives its function and task to be. Moreover, it is a good indication of how much autonomy it has to be what it thinks it should be as a college and university.

Let us recognize that religion *is*: that it *is* studied. And then let us ask whether an institution of higher learning which fails in its curriculum to note these facts is discharging its academic duty. If our answer to this question is negative, then we may get on with the difficult but essential business of asking *how* we may make appropriate provision in our curricula for the study of religious phenomena.

Comments on the Study of Religion

PHILIP H. PHENIX

In a fundamental sense, religion is comprehensive life-orientation. It is therefore relevant to every phase of human experience. It is not a separate compartment of life: a "sacred" area as opposed to other, "secular," areas. This comprehensiveness is most clearly seen in the classic forms of universal religion, such as Hinduism, Buddhism, Judaism, and Christianity. All of these religions in their classic forms have been whole civilizations. All of them had characteristic expressions not only in ritual and in various sacred institutions, but also in art, law, politics, philosophy, and even in science. Religion was the animating principle and the guiding and formative spirit of these comprehensive cultures; the idea of religion as a separate compartment of life was unknown to them. Correspondingly, in the realm of learning, theology was regarded as the "queen of the sciences," the overarching study through which the other forms of knowledge were to be understood and from which, in the final analysis, they were derived.

In modern civilization, however, there is no longer a unifying core and organizing principle. Specialization and differentiation of function are the dominant marks of the secular age. In the university, the consequence has been the development of autonomous disciplines. Or perhaps the university itself has disappeared in all but name, and left in its place is the multiversity. Now, only autonomous disciplines can claim authority and command respect. No one who claims to represent comprehensive life-orientations or synoptic views of all learning dares present himself as a qualified scholar.

One result of this modern development has been the attempt to define religion as a specialized inquiry, one that deals with a limited subject matter: the sacred. This fits in well with the idea of churches as autonomous private associations, analogous to clubs and professional associations. Piety becomes a personal peculiarity, like an interest in the theater or in horse racing. Worship is restricted to certain times and places. Church and state are separated. Religion is regarded as an optional pursuit for people who happen to be interested in that kind of thing, a private affair without any necessary bearing on the main secular concerns of life.

Academically, in the modern multiversity, it is considered absurd

---

The author is professor of philosophy and education at Teachers College, Columbia University.

for anyone to try to deal with everything. Knowledge of everything in general is certainly knowledge of nothing significant at all. The assumption is that one can know only particulars, and thus that one can have only specialized and limited subjects of study. Hence anyone suggesting the study of religion in the multiversity is commonly regarded as proposing the impossible. Furthermore, the old idea that particular truths proceed in deductive fashion from a single authoritative center of revealed wisdom is universally rejected by scholars.

It is interesting to note that the same problems are found in connection with the study of philosophy. Philosophy classically has been thought of as the pursuit of comprehensive wisdom. The outstanding illustration of such a view is the philosophy of Hegel. But today, philosophers have given up the program of speculative construction of world systems; instead, they try to define their work in highly specialized terms through the analysis of language.

It is now becoming clear, however, that differentiation and specialization must be complemented by integration and generalization. Social survival depends on some degree of social co-ordination. As civilization becomes more complex, the need for integration becomes much greater and its achievement more difficult. Even the specialized disciplines themselves depend on integration and generalization for their continued health and progress. Interdisciplinary inquiries promote vigor through cross-fertilization of ideas. In the field of education, for example, general studies which will enable students to gain some sense of the whole enterprise of learning are clearly needed. The schools and colleges are concerned with preparing not only specialists, but also whole persons—persons who have a vivid sense of humane values and of the ways in which the various specialized pursuits fit together in the creation of a good life. The capstone of the educational system should be a true university, a community of scholars who understand one another and see their work within the context of a unified system of values.

Accordingly, there is now room for renewed interest in religion as comprehensive life-orientation. In the context of the present day, religion can be viewed not as a systematic vision from which all particulars can be deduced, but as a comprehensive perspective growing out of the profound consideration of the several specialized disciplines, inductively considered. Religion, seen from this standpoint, is the soul of a culture seeking integral realization. The life of faith grows out of concern for the affairs of real life in the so-called secular world. Many religious thinkers today are emphasizing the need for relevance in religion. This emphasis grows out of an understanding of the contemporary cultural situation and out of the demand for comprehensiveness of commitment and outlook.

According to this view, the distinctive function of religion is the nurture of wholeness. The major goal of the study of religion is to achieve commitment, not only in theoretical understanding, but in a personal and practical way. This concern for wholeness is evident also in the latest developments in philosophy, where mere technical analysis is being superseded by studies of the philosophy of natural science, social science, mathematics, art, morals, history, and other specialized disciplines, with a view to understanding distinctive characteristics, differences, and similarities from discipline to discipline. The integrative aim is also evident in other synoptic studies, such as history, literature, and anthropology, where the narrow confines of one mode of abstraction are surmounted.

How, specifically, can religious studies be carried out so as to nurture wholeness? One obvious way is by the study of the classic religious orientations, which served as the basis for integration in past cultures. This study would normally involve the sympathetic investigation of the historical and literary materials connected with the great religions. The classic orientations would provide the student with models of life-integration for his imaginative exploration.

The other, and perhaps more important, approach to modern religious scholarship in the university would be to study the specialized disciplines in terms of their implicit integral dimensions. For example, language in ultimate perspective may be seen as the word of God, in that the activity of symbolization is a primal human pursuit revealing the centrality of relationship and of spiritual self-transcendence. Science in ultimate perspective may be regarded as the wisdom of God, implicit in the search for truth, the belief in the intelligibility of the world, and the fellowship of persons committed to publicly verifiable understandings. Art in ultimate perspective may be regarded as the work of God, in its concern with the creation of unique objects, in the experience of inspiration, in the enhancement of life by the breaking of traditional molds, and in the incarnation of ideas in material structures. Ethics in ultimate perspective is concerned with the will of God—that is, with response to the author of personal being. History ultimately conceived is the way of God, and the study of history involves a search for meaning and destiny in the human career.

By engaging in the study of the religious dimensions of secular subjects, students can be helped toward personal wholeness, and the living integration of the community of scholars may be advanced, thus creating a real university of inquiry. In turn, such a community may be able to make a substantial contribution to the healing of estrangements and the overcoming of isolation among specialists in the modern world.

The Function of the Study of Religion

Claude Welch

In reviewing the materials distributed in advance for this conference, especially Professor Michaelsen's statement and the report of the Indiana Conference, and in looking over other studies that have emerged in the course of the past fifteen or twenty years, I am struck by the fact that a reasonably broad consensus seems to have developed. The fundamental principles and issues have been hammered out, and it remains for us to interpret them further and to explore ways of implementing them. What I propose to do, therefore, is to set forth informally three summary statements or propositions which may help us with the discussion and which I at least would be prepared to defend.

1. One of the functions or purposes of a college or a university is to provide opportunity for the disciplined, sustained, critical, free study of *all* the domains of human experience.

In spite of (or perhaps because of) the difficulty of formulating a handy definition of religion, it must be affirmed that religion is such a domain. The word refers to multifarious, complex, powerful phenomena that have been close to the center of human experience and culture. In the attitudes, myths and beliefs, codes, and institutions called religious, we deal with man's approaches to ultimate questions: his place in the universe, his final loyalties and loves, the meaning of his existence.

If the fundamental proposition concerning the function of a university is sound, then both the propriety of and the necessity for the study of religion in the university are at once established. However difficult it may be to delimit the scope of reference that the term "religion" (or the "religious") has, the range of experience to which the term directs us is obviously essential for understanding our own past and culture as well as other cultures. This function of the study of religion has long been identified and is now probably beyond the need of serious debate. The question is only one of the proper mode of study.

The first proposition, as I have stated it, also involves the rejection of certain conceptions about what function the study of religion should fulfill. It implies that such study is not carried on for the purposes of evangelism: it is not aimed at persuading students

---

The author is Berg professor and chairman, department of religious thought, University of Pennsylvania.

to adopt any religious or ethical position or posture nor is it intended to "nourish faith." (An educational institution that understands itself to be a direct and explicit organ of a religious community may be an exception to this principle; in such cases, a somewhat different kind of argument would have to be developed, depending upon the self-understanding of that religious community.)

Even though this point may seem perfectly obvious, there has often been serious misunderstanding about it, not least on the part of those who consider themselves friends of the study of religion in the college and the university. Such people have assumed that a department of religion is intended to encourage religion or to cultivate morals. Indirectly, the study of religion as an academic discipline may have such a result, of course; and in the long run, not only may the attempt at an "objective" study of religion develop the student's sensitivities to the kinds of problems with which the religious traditions have been concerned, but also it may serve the best interests of the religious community. The function of the study, however, must not be defined as the care of souls or as catechetical instruction in the faith. And, although no limits can be set on the examination of elements of religious affirmation or on personal expressions of conviction, there should not be any binding of the consciences of students.

On the other hand, the function of the academic study of religion is not that of a unifying or integrating discipline which somehow brings together the whole range of educational experience or most clearly expresses the deepest commitments and convictions of the educational enterprise. Certainly religious traditions are concerned with inclusive goals, universal claims, and fundamental values, and the study of religion will almost certainly engage the student with such questions. But that engagement, understood as the means of integrating education, is not the direct function or purpose of the study.

Similarly, while religious or theological questions (in the sense of questions about ultimate and inclusive goals) are surely involved in the very existence of a university, it is not the task of a department of religion, or of courses in religious studies, to settle these questions. That would be too much to ask of the academic study; moreover, it would mean that the university as a whole had abdicated its responsibilities for dealing with the final questions of its existence.

2. Religion is studied as an academic discipline on the assumption that the domain of experience it treats is available to public scrutiny and that only such experience can be its proper subject matter. In other words, the phenomena to be studied are those that are "in the public domain."

To make this statement is to emphasize the "objectivity" necessary to the study of religion. Objectivity involves appropriateness to the object being studied. Therefore, because the objects of the study of religion include a most personal human act, true objectivity requires sympathy, empathy, imaginative projection, and participation in another's experience. The phenomena direct us to an "interior life of faith," a "being-religious," an act of existing. Thus one must pay the closest attention to statements from internal perspectives: that is, to what is said about the nature of a tradition or a faith by those who take their stand within it.

But that interior act of faith is not itself directly available for study. One cannot say that if the student is to learn or understand what he is supposed to be studying here, he must himself experience the religious faith from within. To put it a little differently, the task is not one of reduplicating in the learner a religious experience or of transmitting an esoteric understanding or truth available only to the "insider." What is available for study, what comes within the range of the phenomena properly dealt with, is only what can be made intelligible and communicated across the line of faith. It is what can be imaginatively understood by the nonbeliever. As Wilfred Cantwell Smith has happily put it, statements (especially about the meaning of a religious tradition) ought properly to be formulated so as to be intelligible in two contexts, that of the man who stands within the community and that of the one who stands outside. Although only the former is able to say, "This is my faith," both must be able to understand.

The principle being affirmed here has yet another consequence. It excludes the "confessional principle" for the teaching of religion. By "confessional principle," I mean the notion that only a Protestant can teach about Protestantism, a Jew about Judaism, a Catholic about Catholicism, a Buddhist about Buddhism, and by implication, a Hegelian about Hegel. As in every other discipline, what may rightfully be asked of the teacher is a commitment to the importance of the subject matter and to the kinds of questions involved. But the confessional principle, as I have defined it, would deny both the public character of the domain we are dealing with and the principle of freedom of inquiry in the university.

3. Religion as an academic discipline is a field of inquiry, a domain, a complex of phenomena, more than a methodology.

If one seeks to defend religion as an academic discipline, one must do so, then, on the grounds that the phenomena are important rather than on the grounds that a single distinctive methodology is involved. Diverse methodologies are essential—linguistic, historical, sociological, psychological, literary, and philosophical.

We come back, then, to the question of characterizing the phenomena. But I trust we shall not bog down on the false quest for a simple definition of "religion." For all the problems that some have had in trying to draw precise limits, it remains clear that the various methodologies can be brought to bear on readily identifiable historical communities (or what W. C. Smith has called "cumulative tradition") and complexes of related phenomena. These traditions and phenomena certainly include ritual activity and liturgy, institutional structures and leadership patterns, sacred writings and objects, statements of belief and mythical expressions, and ethical norms and principles.

Such phenomena can, of course, be studied in other disciplines as well. But if they are to be dealt with adequately, they must also be brought together in a program of study which, just because it seeks to apply diverse methodologies to the given phenomena, is thereby enabled to interpret them more adequately.

At least two general patterns of study, or ways of approach, are indispensable to the discipline and help us to characterize further the nature of the phenomena studied. The two are not exclusive; they are genuinely complementary. (My distinction here corresponds closely to what Professor Michaelsen calls the horizontal and vertical approaches.)

The first approach is that of analyzing types of phenomena commonly called "religious" that may appear in varying forms and shapes in the differing religious traditions. Examples of such phenomena include notions of the "holy community," the distinction between the sacred and the profane, practices of ritual washing, and the myth of the eternal return, to mention but a few.

The second approach is the indispensable study of the historic religious traditions, especially but not exclusively in their development, which includes their contemporary self-understanding. This second kind of study yields perhaps a further principle bearing on the nature of the phenomena that must be dealt with. It has been well formulated recently, by Professor Jacob Neusner of Dartmouth, in the question "Upon what does a given religious tradition focus its best energies?" The answer to such a question provides a natural focus for this second kind of study. In the case of ancient Near Eastern religions, and probably most archaic or primitive religions, this means that the focus will be on mythology and cult. In the case of Judaism, legal and literary development will be emphasized. In the case of Christianity, the student will concentrate on the study of scripture, of sacramental life, and of theology, in varying proportions.

It may not be inappropriate for a professional theologian, one whose title is "professor of religious thought," to conclude by noting not only the possibility but the necessity of studying theology within the phenomena appropriate to religion as an academic discipline. In this way, we may emphasize the importance of studying the self-understanding of a religious community, as well as the special significance of theological endeavors for such traditions as Christianity. The range of appropriateness extends not only to the history of theology or to contemporary theology, but also to such studies as "fundamentals of Catholic theology" or even to the systematic explication of constructive theological positions by those persons who are themselves engaged in their formulation.

The Context and Structure of Religion as an Academic Discipline

The Nature and Formulation of Academic Disciplines

Richard Schlatter

The title I have been given is one of those vague and abstract phrases which I associate with the administrative mind—a type of mind which I can never take very seriously. I suppose I am an administrator, but I like to think of myself as an historian and a humanist, and I never think about administration in the abstract.

Concretely, I suppose that what we are talking about—or what I am supposed to be leading up to—is whether religion should or should not be organized as a department in the university. Professor Michaelsen has said in his pamphlet on *The Scholarly Study of Religion* that "the question . . . is not *whether* to study religion, but *how* to study it." I take it we all agree with that statement in general.

He goes on to say that religion in the university should involve an undergraduate major and graduate work and that the "curriculum should be under the direction of a department, or some similar administrative structure, which would give it the same status (faculty rank, financial support, etc.) as other departments." The most recent annual report of the Danforth Foundation says, "Everyone agrees that we need departments of religion, if religion is to be properly dealt with in colleges and universities." Perhaps there is not complete agreement in this matter—in academia there is never complete agreement on anything, thank God. But I would not wish to quarrel with Professor Michaelsen on this; he is, after all, the most persuasive advocate, and perhaps the most successful organizer, of departments of religion in the country. Still, I might just ask the question, "If the matter is really decided, why are we still talking about it?"

Let me begin by making two plain statements about my own opinions in this matter of departments of religion.

First, I agree with Professor Michaelsen and the Danforth Foundation that if the study of religion is to flourish in the university, it should be established as a department just like economics or chemistry or history or sociology.

Second, in my own university, I have been most reluctant to proceed with the organization of departments of religion in the five undergraduate colleges of liberal arts and in the graduate school of

---

The author is provost and vice president of Rutgers—The State University of New Jersey.

arts and sciences with its six liberal arts faculties. In fact, we already have a department of religion in one of these undergraduate colleges: namely, in Douglass, the women's college. It is not without significance, I think, that the women's college should be the home of our only religion department; it's generally conceded that in modern America women are the more conventionally pious and the more given to religiosity. Certainly the course in religious ethics, which is advertised in the Douglass catalogue as "a study of the relevance of Judeo-Christian ethics for conduct in courtship," seems especially designed to protect the virtue of our young ladies.

These, then, are my two points: (1) in theory, I think religion will be shamefully neglected unless it is housed in a department in the university; and (2) in practice, I am not anxious to have departments of religion in my own university.

What I have to say about the nature and formulation of academic disciplines has been said before and the relevance of these remarks to the study of religion has been referred to by a number of authorities. There is Professor Michaelsen himself; and then there is the very full summary of most of the arguments in Clyde Holbrook's *Religion, a Humanistic Field*, one of the volumes in the Princeton Studies in Humanistic Scholarship. "The modern university," Holbrook points out, "builds its educational program on the departmental system."

I need not spend time on the faults inherent in organizing universities, and knowledge itself, into disciplines. We all know that in large universities, where the individual departments have huge staffs and even separate buildings, professors of English speak only to professors of English, physicists to physicists, and so on. This situation is often disastrous for the education of undergraduates; the chemist sees every undergraduate only as a potential chemist, the sociologist thinks every student intends to become a professional sociologist, and no one is concerned about the student who wants a liberal or general education—even the terms are unfashionable nowadays. No one is concerned about students as human beings. These facts are well known, and all over the country large universities are trying to break up departmental divisions at the undergraduate level and to persuade highly specialized professors that they should be, at least part of the time, teachers who are responsible for the total education of young men and women. Sometimes the mathematician should remember that most of the students in the freshman math course will never take any more math and will forget all the math that he is teaching them there—and so on in sociology, history, philosophy, and all the other departments.

We at Rutgers are in the process of founding three new coeducational colleges in New Brunswick. We chose to do this rather than to expand the present colleges because we want to dissolve, for the purposes of undergraduate education, what I think are our excessive departmental loyalties. We hope that every member of the faculty will recognize two loyalties: that to his departmental discipline—which is the only one he recognizes now—and that to his college as an institution which is interested in more than just the professional education of its students. We are not going so far as the University of California at Santa Cruz, which is abolishing departments altogether at the college level and restricting the traditional organization by discipline to the graduate level. Whether Santa Cruz will succeed or not is an open question. At Rutgers, where the departments are entrenched, armed to the teeth, and spoiling for a fight, we would not dare undertake anything so revolutionary. We may even fail in our more modest plan of enlarging the faculty's loyalties to the institution as a whole. But we propose to make the attempt.

Departments, then, can impose harmful limitations on the education of undergraduates. Perhaps a more serious consequence of the separation among academic disciplines is the injury inflicted on the life of the mind, on the development of a rich and critical scholarship and fruitful scientific research. Departmentalization fosters more and more specialization, more and more pedantry, and more and more triviality. We all know, in the abstract, that much of the most original scholarship and research arises just in those border areas where traditional disciplines rub together and generate sparks of new knowledge. Every university administrator knows that he must foster interdisciplinary research centers and institutes: chemists must have a place set aside where they can talk to biologists; historians and sociologists and psychologists must somehow communicate with one another if their disciplines are to flourish and grow in depth; and we must bring a host of specialists from various departments together if we are to make any headway in solving the appalling problems of our big cities.

Nevertheless, every administrator knows also that such research centers and institutes are a headache. Much of the time, the various specialists who sit together in the interdisciplinary research institute resemble nothing so much as the emissaries of enemy powers negotiating an uneasy cease-fire. Each one is jealous of the rights and privileges and prerogatives and budgetary independence of his discipline. Everyone thinks that joint appointments between two or more departments are a good thing, but the man who holds one may find himself in a no man's land where promotions are hard to come by. Departments rule the roost in the American university and will, I believe, for a long time to come. And, I would add, I do not wish to see them unduly weakened. For the strong position of the department in the modern American university is not merely a historical accident, and their prestige is not solely a matter of prescriptive right and vested interest and entrenched privilege. They do, after all, have an intellectual justification.

Without departments, the intellectual establishment would be disordered and amateurish. The organization by discipline fosters a needed specialization and a concentration of intellectual effort. Only when we move from the natural philosopher through the virtuoso or amateur scientist to the biologist and then to the microbiologist do we make rapid progress in knowledge. In spite of the limitations which we all recognize, the organization of our intellectual establishments of higher learning along disciplinary lines has been a success and continues to be a success. We should break down the fences at some points; we should redraw the boundaries from time to time; and we may want to create new disciplines. But we need the disciplines all the same. They have justified themselves in practice.

In addition, we usually maintain that each of the disciplines has an internal coherence, a method of investigation, a methodology, which justifies its existence by distinguishing it theoretically. Mathematicians do think mathematically, historians supposedly think historically, and so on. In recent years, specialization within disciplines has increased so rapidly that methodological coherence between the various specialties has sometimes dissolved; and it has always been true that the scholarly method of the historians of the ancient world, for example, differs greatly from the method of the historians of the recent past. But although the definitions of the disciplines according to their differing methodologies have not been very precise, we have grown accustomed to talk of the method of each of the great families—science, social science, and humanities—and of the individual disciplines within these families. The definitions and the boundaries are never agreed upon and they never stay put, but they seem to represent some logical and practically useful way to classify our knowledge.

Well, then, what of religion? Practically, since the departmental disciplines are the power centers of our universities, unless the study of religion is organized in a department, that study will be shortchanged and neglected. The founding of departments of religion in so many colleges and universities in the last twenty-five years reflects the determination of scholars to establish the study and teaching of religion on grounds of independent, intellectual equality with other disciplines. Unless such a subject has the status and dignity of a departmental organization, students will conclude that the subject is of little intellectual importance. Without a department and without a major program which a department makes possible, the teacher of religion is reduced to a general service function which derogates his dignity and deadens his own intellectual growth. Concretely, the study of religion will get its share of the budget only if it has the status of a department. This is the practical argument for a department of religion. It is a powerful one.

I have said that, in a rather vague and imprecise way, the disciplines are supposed to have some internal coherence, some distinguishing methodology. Does the study of religion have such an internal logic of its own? Professor Michaelsen writes, "The really crucial question is whether or not religion will be fully recognized as an academic discipline." We could rephrase the question and ask not whether religion *will be recognized* as an academic discipline but whether religion in fact *is* an academic discipline.

I cannot attempt to answer that question. But let me list some considerations which will affect any answer we give.

1. History, economics, modern literature, psychology, political science—all of these are solid disciplines in the modern university; yet each had to fight its way into the curriculum against the opposition of those who said they had no distinctive methodologies. Thus we should be suspicious when we are told that studies in religion have no methodological coherence.

2. Surely studies in religion are as unified now as sociology, a study of which it has recently been said that as soon as a man becomes respectably proficient in it, he ceases to call himself a sociologist and becomes a historian, an anthropologist, a demographer, or some such, because there is no such thing as sociology.

3. A very real problem in setting up departments of religion is, as Professor Michaelsen says, the availability of qualified staff. We want scholar-teachers, but what we have available is a roster of liberal Protestant apologists and evangelists with an occasional Jew or Jesuit thrown in to make it appear respectably broad-minded.

I don't want to labor the problem of indoctrination—we all know about it. I think it is still a major problem. Too many teachers of religion come either from Protestant seminaries or from university departments of religion which are, in tone and outlook, parts of the Protestant Establishment. One department opens its departmental meetings with prayer; in another, a Catholic teacher becomes converted to Protestantism; I know of no department which attracts as students any reasonable proportion of Catholics or orthodox Jews—a matter of considerable political importance for us at state universities in the East.

4. On the matter of who is a qualified scholar in religion and what should be taught in the department of religion, Professor Michaelsen seems to me to adopt the very views which make it impossible for religion to assume a proper place in the university. He wants for his teachers saints who can get at the meaning of religion from within, in ways which an outsider might not fully understand. As a practical matter, I would prefer not to have any saints on my faculty—difficult men and women to deal with; and if we do not have to have Marxists to teach Marxism, or ancient Greeks to expound paideia, why must we have saints to teach religion?

In fact, if a scholar's religious convictions lead him to assume that no one can understand a given document unless he accepts it as revelation, then such a scholar should join the faculty of a sectarian institution and not try to teach in the secular and state universities, where the majority of his students will not be able to accept his assumption. If the study of religion is to be established as a department which will enjoy the respect of scholar-teachers, it must break away from the narrow views which still prevail. It must stop being a part of the Protestant Establishment, it must stop defining religion as Christianity, and liberal Protestant Christianity at that. And it must stop talking about revelation as if there were only one revelation, or as if all men agreed as to what that one is. Professor Michaelsen says that "one need not be 'religious' in order to appreciate the importance of the subject, any more than one need be an artist to appreciate art as an aspect of culture." I would extend that to read that "one need not be 'religious' in order to study and teach religion, any more than one need be an artist to study and teach art as an aspect of culture."

We must rid ourselves of evangelical parochialism. Even a meeting such as the one which we had in 1964 at Indiana reminds me a little bit of the camp meetings which my Methodist preacher grandfather took me to in Ohio as a boy—there seems to be a tone of pious zeal which is not present in conferences on the organization of urban studies or the studio arts or some other subject struggling for recognition in the university.

The teaching of religion must, in the state university, be an academic subject, taught by scholars who have mastered a discipline. It should be separated entirely from efforts to lift and maintain the religious tone of the campus.

The study of religion is too important to be left in the hands of the religious.

The Scholarly Study of Religion in College and University

Thomas F. O'Dea

Perhaps the best way that I can approach the problem of the scholarly study of religion in colleges and universities is to talk against the background of my own current experience in a very new academic position as chairman of the department of religion at Columbia University. First of all, what I say here represents chiefly my own point of view, but it is one which in its most important parts, at least, is, I believe, in general agreement with the views of my colleagues who are in that department or associated with it. Second, I will discuss the problem of a department of religion without questioning the current organization of the university. Vice-President Schlatter's comments about the difficulties involved in the departmentalization of the university are well worth our reflection and thought, and I have reflected and thought about them for some time. I find myself, nonetheless, working in a department and now beginning to chair one. Third, my remarks will be concerned more with graduate than with undergraduate education. Again, this is partly an accident of my current situation, since our department at the moment is engaged in trying to rethink the graduate program.

What I'm concerned with here is the objective, scholarly study of religion, not with any form of evangelization, whether overt or subtle. The very term "teaching religion" is an ambiguous one, since most of us were brought up to understand by that term indoctrination in a particular religion. But as I see it, the aim of the college or university courses in religion is the objective scholarly study of religion. Now I am aware, quite aware, of the difficulties inherent in the word "objective," I take it to mean the attempt to understand the ideational content, the cultural context, and the social situation of particular religions—Western and non-Western—both historically and at the present time. It's true, of course, that in trying to achieve objectivity, we approach from certain cultural and even disciplinary perspectives. And it's also true that here below one does not achieve the over-all objectivity that the philosopher ascribes as characteristic of the mind of God. But we do attempt to overcome certain of the limitations of our perspective, to break through them in some way. We do try to suspend our prejudices. We do try to understand what the material is saying, and to understand it in several contexts.

The author is professor and chairman, department of religion, Columbia University.

The first and fundamental reason for the study of religion in the college and university is to gain some comprehension of the role of religion in human life and history. A second, and very important, reason is to increase our understanding of man and the changing form of his awareness, his relationships, and his strivings. I am approaching the study of religion in the same way that the departmentalized areas of the humanities and social sciences presumably approach their subject matter. As has been suggested already, academic departments or academic disciplines imply in many cases a particular and peculiar methodology. This, of course, is more true in the ideal than it is in fact. The historian, for example, must know a good deal about a number of things if he is to write the history of various fields. It would not do for a historian to write the history of physics in American universities over the past twenty-five years if he is unaware of the content of physics, and the same principle holds true for many of the other social sciences. In the study of religion, method, I believe, means focusing the typical methodologies and techniques of several disciplines—history, psychology, philosophy, sociology, and textual studies being the chief ones that come to my mind—upon the substantive field of religion. And I define the field, as I think all academic disciplines did in the beginning, in a common-sense, denotative manner. That is, I point to behavior and attitudes which we characterize in our everyday discussions as being religious and I regard them as the objects of our study. I will concede that as points of view become more profound and more sophisticated, the difference between the study of religion, in the kind of setting which I have suggested, and the study of certain types of political ideologies may diminish, or even disappear. But I start with the common-sense understanding of what is meant by religion.

When these disciplines are focused upon religion, they themselves, or their techniques and methodologies, may undergo a change, a broadening, a transformation. More is involved than mere technique. The sociologist, in looking at religion, finds that he must become aware of the content of religion: its belief content, its attitudinal content, and its history. And he must become aware to an extent and a degree that would not be demanded of him if he had remained a sociologist functioning in an average sociology department.

So although we may not be able to speak of the study of religion as having a method in the way that an ideal—though seldom an actual—academic department may be said to have a method, still we can refer to it as a discipline. The focusing of the methods and the points of view of the five fields upon the subject matter of religion requires the development of a methodological perspective which will affect the development of techniques.

So far I have touched upon the aim of the university study of religion, the reason such study is worthwhile, and some of the methodological considerations relating to religion as an academic discipline. Now I would like to turn to the question of organization. Professor Michaelsen has said, and I think it can hardly be questioned, that the development of a discipline requires that there be organized in some form a corps of specialists working upon the subject matter. If religion is a peripheral concern, scattered among literature departments, history departments, sociology departments, then it will remain peripheral and any focus upon it will be the choice of an individual. Lacking an organized corps, there will be little opportunity for the kind of exchange, dialogue, and debate which the development of scholarship requires. Therefore I assume that the carrying out of the aim requires some form of organization of the corps of scholars and social scientists who are involved.

The question then arises as to what form such organization should take—that of a department or that of an interdepartmental committee of some kind. In the abstract, much can be said on both sides of this question. Concretely, it often comes down to the situation in the particular college or university. There are advantages in the central focus as well as in the legitimation which the establishment of a department provides. However, in a deeper sense, certain fundamental problems remain the same. Whether one has a department or an interdepartmental committee, what is involved remains an interdisciplinary venture.

In the department of religion at Columbia, for example, we have as adjunct professors on our faculty a number of people in other departments—in history, public law, the studies of ancient Near Eastern and Middle Eastern cultures. In addition to having these professors as adjuncts, we offer, as part of our program, courses in other departments which fulfill certain needs of our students. We also have a joint program at the Union Theological Seminary, a number of whose faculty are adjunct professors in our department. We have, as a matter of fact, about a half-a-dozen men working full time in the department, plus about twenty adjunct professors from the Union Theological Seminary and from other parts of the university. So the interdepartmental character of the venture is not really changed by having the study of religion set up as a department. The advantage to having a department, as Vice-President Schlatter has indicated—over and above the respectability it confers and even the space that is allotted to a department is, of course, that this is one way of legitimating the venture financially in the structure of the university, of getting money allocated for the study of religion.

Finally, I would like to consider the problem of selecting an emphasis. "Religion" is a term that covers a great deal of ground.

The history and theory of religion indicate a very broad field to be studied, and every department of religion must make some choice of emphasis. The choice has to be made, I believe, in two areas. One is that of substance: Will the department concentrate on the Judeo-Christian stream in Western religion? Will it concentrate on some of the non-Western religious traditions? Or will it try to work out some manageable combination of the two? This last possibility is not without its dangers. It would be regrettable if five or six departments of religion in leading universities were developed, and they all competed against each other in the various subfields of religion. For example, if we were to compete against each other for a Buddhologist in America today, I can assure you that some departments would have to do without one, because there just aren't enough to go around. The problem of working out some kind of division of labor among the universities is an important one. Thus we have the question of emphasis in terms of substance.

But there is also the problem of emphasis in terms of discipline. I have used the term "the history and theory of religion," but the individual department must decide for itself which emphasis it wishes to take. Is it to become known chiefly for the history of religion? For the sociology of religion? For textual criticism in Biblical studies or in non-Western religion? For the psychology of religion—a much neglected but very important field in our time, though it elicits little interest from academic psychologists? I am suggesting that there is a kind of core which the department can look on as characteristic of itself and can try to build around. Certainly if a department attempts to cover a whole field, to be too generalized, it will lack depth and genuine scholarship. Some of the problems here involve specialization versus generalization, substance versus analysis. Each department must work out its own proper mix in view of its peculiar situation, its resources and potential resources, the traditions of the university, the needs of its staff, and the like.

Finally, why university graduate study in religion? Simply because if the university is dedicated to the examination of life, then it must be concerned with the examination of religion. To allow a seminary to have a monopoly in the study of religion is to invite a certain amount of bias and incompleteness. What is needed is that such study be related to the general study of man as it is carried out in the humanities and in the social sciences. Only in this way can the consideration of the role of religion in human life assume its rightful place among the liberal arts.

Reflections on Michaelsen's *Scholarly Study of Religion*

BENJAMIN NELSON

During the week preceding this conference, I found myself writing several statements on this evening's subject. One of these was intended to serve as a sort of personal testimonial in behalf of Dr. Michaelsen's view that the scholarly interest in the study of religion in college and university needs to be greatly expanded. More recently, however, as I was having a fresh look at the latter part of Dr. Michaelsen's paper, I belatedly discovered in it an elision between two related but surely not identical notions, the notion of "the scholarly study of religion" and the notion of "religion as an academic discipline." Then and there I found myself wanting to add another section to my remarks, one somewhat less positive and more problematical in tone than my first drafts.

The result of all this juggling is that as I have been listening to the speakers who have preceded me, I have found myself having to perform several sleights of hand. Now, as my turn has come to speak to the issues before us, I have decided that it would be best, after all, if I began, as initially planned, with my positive endorsement of the call for an increase in "the scholarly study of religion."

The personal tone of this statement should not be taken to mean that I subscribe to present-day philosophical pronouncements which call for total "authenticity" at any price. My main purpose is a more modest one—to offer a case study in the form of a life history. "Clinical" reports and flesh-and-bones "life-histories" of this sort need to be gathered before we can recapture the neglected inner life of university communities and of each group of its inhabitants. We need to know much more than we do about the ways in which faculties and students respond to the alternative maps of knowledge and mappings of culture.

I refer to maps and mappings in order to provide a wider context for understanding the issues posed here. So far as I can tell, there is no society anywhere in the world which is not in some way forced to evolve some schema, a cultural system, as we now say, which serves a complex of functions. One of these functions is to provide a dramatic design, giving the appearance of aim, purpose, significance, and consequence to passing occasions. Only in this way

---

The author was professor of sociology at the State University of New York at Stony Brook and is now on the faculty of the New School for Social Research.

can objects and events which may actually lack an unambiguous or intrinsic aim achieve the appearance of meaning. A second function is illustrated in the fact that every society known to us evolves one or another schema for promoting conformity to its central purposes through what I call directive system. (I know of no communication, including the one that I am now involved in with you, which does not, in fact, prompt us to think, see, believe, feel, in one way rather than in another.)

Finally, I would observe that every society also develops a symbol economy: that is, a scheme whereby all possible values which men prize are produced and distributed. Whatever the scheme be, it seems that men have disputed—and will dispute—with one another over what they consider their fair share of the symbolic income.

I must continue for a while longer in this vein even at the risk of sounding like that sort of sociologist not usually regarded with favor by historians: I have elsewhere sought to discriminate six classes of cues which, taken together, make up the central directive programs of the culture. For reasons of economy, I use Latin gerunds to name the different categories of cues:

Percipienda—The cues defining in what ways and how any events, objects, situations are to be perceived. These constitute the central frames of reference of a culture.

Sentienda—The cues telling us what and how we must feel

Agenda—The cues defining what we must do or avoid doing

Credenda—The cues defining what requires to be believed and professed

Miranda—The cues establishing what and whom we must hold in awe

Emulanda—The cues establishing whom we are charged to emulate

I have further sought to show that the cues within any of the classes, and, indeed, the relationship among the classes of cues themselves, must be tolerably consistent, tolerably stable, tolerably congruent with individual and social experience, however these experiences be derived.

It is, indeed, not possible for individuals or social groups to function well if the components of the directive programs are, as it were, out of phase. In Durkheim's terms, society runs the risk of *anomie* whenever:

(1) The actors—social groups as well as individuals—are unable to find a compelling center in the cues;

(2) The directive programs forfeit the assent and respect of individuals because of the chasm between the rewards promised and the rewards reserved for conformity to the system;

(3) Evident improprieties exist in the distribution of means to prized value;

(4) Men find themselves unable to establish appropriate identifications and effective identities because of a lack of connection between the proclaimed values of persons and their own sense of fitness.

How are these overarching perspectives relevant to the issues before us? One main implication of what I am saying is that the problem of locating religion as a collegiate study cannot be resolved without making certain assumptions as to the scope and mission of the university. If the cosmos once called the university had not drifted toward the chaos called the multiversity, we might not be in such great need as we are of intensifying the scholarly study of religion in higher educational institutions. With growing frequency, one or another social or group function is dropped in the lap of institutions or agents not originally charged with primary responsibility for them. Colleges and universities provide decisive instances of this process: In recent days, they have been asked to undertake many new complex tasks because other social units and their agents have proved unwilling or unable to perform their traditional functions. The main challenge now, when the university's own mind is so greatly out of joint, is to find the appropriate place in the university curriculum for interests formerly served by religion. Our students do not want to know about our difficulties in making up our minds, nor can they accept as final the fact that, to recall the poet's words, "things are in the saddle . . . and whirl is King."

The events of our times are working at cross purposes. On the one hand, we are required to be more attentive than we have ever been to the questions we are discussing at this conference. These questions now have an urgency that they have not had in any age since the French Revolution. When the incomparable Max Weber died in 1920, it was possible for sociologists of religion to imagine that the issues with which Weber was dealing—the roots, sources, development, and organization of the distinctively modern Western society and culture—were issues principally to be decided by specialized historians of the Middle Ages and the Reformation. But today it is apparent, as it could not have been before, that Weber's fertile hypotheses were yet to receive their ultimate test around the whole world in the crucible of the process of development. Wherever modernization occurs, extraordinary religious developments associated with reform and revolution occur. We must understand these developments if we are to survive as a civilization. The study of contemporary religion has a poignancy that it has not had for centuries.

One of the main gaps I found in Dr. Michaelsen's paper is that throughout his remarks about understanding the great traditions, he seems always to be thinking in terms of a finished past, and a consensus among experts as to its character. But Dr. Michaelsen has not given sufficient weight to the unforeseen revolutionary changes which have been occurring in the organization and the belief systems of religions at every level of development. A decade ago, no one could have predicted that the surrogate religion known as revolutionary Marxism would pass from the West, where it was born, to the Far East, where it had no precedents; the Chinese Communists have now inherited the apostolic succession and the deposit of the original faith. Who could have guessed that the supposedly unchanging Roman Catholic Church would be subject to so remarkable a series of spurs to modernization as it has since the beginning of Pope John XXIII's reign? The extraordinary thrust of the messianic "religions of the oppressed" in Africa, Asia, and Latin America has given an entirely new dimension to our times. We are today in the middle of some of the most dramatic changes in the religious sphere which have ever occurred in the history of man. If we overlook this point, our response to the issues which confront us at this conference will be confused.

Now to my promised testimonial. I will not try to explain how, at a relatively tender age, before I had even entered upon my undergraduate career, I had come to realize that both our institutions and our behavior were destined to remain wrapped in mystery unless we first made contact with the deeper strata of inherited meaning which lay beneath the surface trivialities of the daily round. The study of the Middle Ages, the Renaissance, and the Reformation soon seemed to me a fountainhead where, if I exerted myself to the utmost, I might come into touch with structures of meaning and modes of organization which promised to be the key to many riddles of our times.

Even as an undergraduate, I came to realize that the scholarly study of religion was not to be expected in the undergraduate college except as a chance phenomenon. I also found that there were a number of reasons—not given enough weight in Dr. Michaelsen's paper—for the evident inability of many otherwise outstanding academic institutions to relate intelligently to the role of religion in history and in the conduct of life.

My first observation was that access to the roots and broader meanings of the major historic societies and religions was cut off at the source because a great number of teachers had a powerful commitment to a set of doctrines much less subtle than the theologies with which I was only then coming into contact. Two of these newer doctrines call for special mention: One was "faith in reason": that is, the *faith* that reason is the force that guarantees inevitable, irreversible progress. The second doctrine saw history as the successive elimination of irrational restraints in a sequence of *revolutions* beginning with the so-called Renaissance and continuing, as we have been taught, with the Protestant Reformation, the scientific revolution of the seventeenth century, a sequence of political revolutions (the English Revolution, the American Revolution, and the French Revolution), and capped by a series of industrial revolutions culminating in the technological and scientific triumphs of our atomic age.

The more carefully I came to study these materials, the more I came to see that this way of telling the story was really not scientific history so much as picture-book mythology supported by a mystique which had come into being largely because our culture lacked compelling dramatic designs or frames by which persons could readily locate themselves in the cosmos. The two faiths—faith in reason and faith in history—were hardly less dramatic in tone than the thirteenth- and fourteenth-century doctrines I had been assigned to study as a beginning graduate student.

Soon, also, I was to discover that many American medievalists were committed to a series of presuppositions which, whether justified on pragmatic grounds or by considerations of a more philosophical nature, led them to deny that the Middle Ages, the Renaissance, and the Reformation had any connection whatever with the religious life. I was to be told that the Middle Ages were not a bit less secular than our own age, nor medieval men any the less controlled by purely worldly motivations than ourselves. Heresy was not doctrinal or religious in any important sense, but was rather an instance of the self-assertion of the confident middle classes who would not accept the ecclesiastical restraints on the freedom of enterprise. Theology, I was to be advised, must be kept separated from philosophy. Medieval philosophy could be studied without having recourse to the history of religious experience or theological development. The Jews in the Middle Ages were not to be studied, a distinguished professor explained, from a "lachrymose point of view," and their history was simply a part of the general social and cultural development of man. The more I immersed myself in primary sources, the more questionable these suppositions appeared to me. It did not take very long, moreover, before the catastrophic events in the world at large exposed the shaky foundation on which these faiths had been reared.

As change dictated, the era of our civilization's greatest agony found me working among the ruins in the hope of finding truer ways of charting the development of sensibility, ideals, and institutions in the western world. Concentrating on documentary remains too long neglected, I successively studied the ways in which the ecclesiastical laws concerning restitution of usurious or ill-gotten gains bear upon the activities of men on the high seas, in the market place, and in the courts; the changes in the images of brother, neighbor, friend from the days of the Hebrew prophets to our own time; the workings of the ideas and institutions connected with the regulation of conscience, casuistry, and the cure of souls; the shifts in the self-images and the systems of self-direction down to our own day. Wherever I turned, I found myself having to clear away a debris of ideological clichés inherited from the rationalist and historicist past. Those teachers who weren't controlled by what I have described as "historiosophic" myth and mystique of the triumph of reason were controlled by other equally questionable assumptions, such as the view that everything always remains fundamentally the same.

I turn now to a second experience of my career which I think increasingly describes our situation today. There are many universities not characterized by the blend of secular myths and mystiques I have described above. In them, a slightly different situation prevails: One is at a loss to find his way through the labyrinth of unrelated studies which somehow come to find a place in the multiversity. Here my studies of conscience, casuistry, and the cure of souls helped to recognize neglected facts.

Every one of the disciplines which we now view as a separate science can be shown to have emerged from a historical matrix of one or another sort. Most of the issues which came to prove a ruling interest of my life emerged, as it was to appear, out of the matrix of law, morality, and logic more recently than most people suppose. I freely grant that knowledge has been advanced by the disengagement of separate subject matters from the original matrix. Each is now given absolute liberty to pursue its own problems in accordance with its own lights. At the same time, I cannot overlook the cost side of the ledger. Today's multiversities and higher educational communities suffer from anarchy bordering on *anomie*. Great numbers of specialists are unable to recognize the source of the problems, the foundations of their theories, and the inferences which may legitimately be deduced from their findings. The gravity of this problem is growing by leaps and bounds.

Wherever I have been, I have seen the university caught up in agonizing struggles of the soul; and whenever I really look closely, I inevitably find that the struggle is in no sense purely or even mainly scientific. It is really a kind of religious and even theological struggle. I dare not do more than suggest that a rationalism prevails which challenges all varieties of historicism, biologism, socialism. Reason, it is assumed, can instantly provide answers to any and all the problems which time and circumstance generate. Opposed to this is a brute empiricism which treats reason as epiphenomenal.

On another campus, these two options were put in entirely different terms. Here the one and only issue was whether the issues admitted of a scientific analysis. If they did not, "raw feel" was allowed to run its course undisturbed by the intrusion of scientific modes. Opposed to *pure scientism* was *instant existentialism,* which lodged mainly in the department of English.

Enough has been said to suggest how many obstacles stand in the way of developing an agreed-on map of knowledge. Everywhere one goes, the options constitute a different spectrum. Today the indications for maps are extremely confusing.

The implications of these observations should not be allowed to elude us. On many campuses, the scholarly study of religion fails to make strides because of the enveloping urgency of surrogate theologies. We allow ourselves to miss this fact because the polemics innocently masquerade as arguments about the methods and mission of science. Wherever the apocalyptic spirit of scientism permeates the atmosphere, there is little place for the scholarly study either of religion or of the moral life.

Returning to my initial point, I find myself in great sympathy with Dr. Michaelsen's proposal with regard to the promotion and advancement of the scholarly study of religion. I think everybody aspiring to be fully human needs to give himself to the scrupulous study of religious experience and expression in human history.

The latter part of Dr. Michaelsen's paper, however, poses difficulties which admit of no easy resolution. Provost Schlatter has already suggested some of the more perplexing problems. I believe that the words "religion as an academic discipline" raise many other issues as well. To explore Dr. Michaelsen's second notion is to open Pandora's box. If religion is to be an *academic* discipline it must be *academic* in the historic sense of that phrase—free of partisan control, open to radical doubt, responsive to every turn of the spirit, however wayward. A discipline which is not academic in this sense easily becomes a halter. The study of religion as a scholarly subject proceeds on the assumption that "the spirit bloweth where it listeth." Who would want a separate academic discipline which rested on a different assumption? I am confident that Dr. Michaelsen would not want that.

The Study of Religion:
A Family of Academic Disciplines

JOHN F. WILSON

We have been asked to make our statements both brief and weighty. Consequently, my contribution will take the form of four propositions. Under cross-examination, I might not be prepared to defend each in the form that I express it. Sharply drawn statements, however, may have value in provoking serious discussion.

An earlier version of the conference agenda defined my task as justifying the study of religion as a discrete discipline—that is to say, a discipline *sui generis*. I do not think that it is a discipline *sui generis*, but I do think it is a legitimate family of disciplines, and what I have to say will tend toward that conclusion.

Initially we must have very clearly in view what we mean by the "study of religion" or "religion as an academic discipline." At the risk of artificiality, I think it is helpful to distinguish between three different kinds of study of religion which might be sponsored within a contemporary university. Parenthetically, I recognize that no actual institution may embody these alternatives, singly or in combination, but I think it is important to recognize them as ideal distinctions. First, the study of religion may be carried on primarily under a "faculty of theology." A faculty of theology is predicated upon, and its object in view is, either a body of alleged revelation or a tradition of religious life. The intention of that faculty is to further explore the revelation or tradition, assuming them to be "true." The second kind of study of religion in a contemporary university would be a "school of religion." Essentially this is an institution dedicated to the practical study of religion and the training of religious functionaries; a school of forestry or a school of nursing has an analogous purpose. Thus a school of religion would be primarily concerned, I should think, with educating religious workers or making accessible to university students a useful and practical knowledge of a religious tradition or traditions. The third general kind of study of religion would be within the faculty of arts and sciences, or what has been called the "philosophical faculty." The object in view for this third kind of study of religion is the manifold religious life of the human species, or that class of phenomena labeled religious; the intention is to analyze it as a coherent aspect of human culture.

The author is assistant dean of the college and assistant professor of religion at Princeton University.

While I do not wish to push these distinctions too far, it is very important to be clear that in this conference we are talking primarily about the study of religion within an arts and sciences faculty, or, by extension, within a liberal arts college. My initial proposition then is simply the following: if we rigorously distinguish the study of religion under the arts and sciences faculty from the work of a faculty of theology on the one hand, or of a school of religion on the other, most of the prevailing uncertainties about what the study of religion is are resolved, and many of the prejudices against it are proved groundless.

My second proposition is a consequence of the first one. Currently there are three prominent models or patterns for developing the study of religion within colleges and universities; not only are these models seductive but, more important, they are grounded in one or another fundamental error.

1. The first of these models is primarily concerned with the study of religion as an aspect of the humanities. It is argued that the humanities are incomplete unless direct attention is given to the religious sources of human values; without that attention, the humanities have lost what is central to them. The study of religion may even be implicitly defined as the *sine qua non* of liberal education.

The study of religion shaped on this model is predicated upon a serious misunderstanding about the humanities: namely, that "liberal education" is primarily to be identified with the "humanities." It is assumed that the purpose of liberal education is to "humanize" the student, to create in him humane values. Liberal education, however, properly includes not only study of the subjects we know as the humanities, but also study of the natural sciences and social sciences. Liberal education properly disciplines the intellect of the student in the arts and the sciences and, with regard to his values, seeks an uncoerced response. It does not mold him to a pattern provided by one conception of the humanities. The study of religion when shaped on this model, therefore, is based upon a gross oversimplification of the genuine richness and vitality which must characterize a liberal education and a faculty of arts and sciences. To put it metaphorically, the faculty of arts and sciences of a university or the college faculty granting a liberal arts degree is more like the shifting patterns seen through a kaleidoscope than the beam of light focused by a lens or the spectrum refracted by a prism. No one subject, including religion, can be defined as central to the humanities; and the humanities, however conceived, do not define liberal education. Incidentally, study of religion shaped on this model obscures the social reality of religion.

2. The second unfortunate model upon which study of religion is currently based constitutes a response to the religious pluralism of our society. The study of religion is often shaped on the principle

of "representing" within the college curriculum the primary religious options within our society. In the extreme case, proponents of this model argue that we should have representatives of Protestantism teaching about Protestant Christianity, representatives of Roman Catholicism teaching about Roman Catholic Christianity and, of course, bona fide members of the Jewish community teaching about the Jewish tradition. It is hoped that, in relation to each other, these men will also "represent" ecumenism and interfaith dialogue.

This model is specious because it assumes that a university or a college is not very different from a zoo; the principle of representing species is also appropriate to a museum. It is hardly a principle appropriate for structuring the curriculum of a higher educational institution or for selecting its faculty. Imagine the study of politics being based upon the principle of representation! One would include, I suppose, communists, socialists, nationalists, consensus Democrats and Republicans, conservative Republicans, and far-right-wingers. A responsible student of politics would throw up his hands in despair at such a proposal.

There is, perhaps, an additional reason why the study of religion has been constructed upon this model: Because religions (at least, those that are dogmatic) seek proselytes, it seems proper for the subject to be taught by advocates of these religions. If we have in mind the distinctions offered in my first proposition, however, we will recognize the faulty logic in this kind of proposal. Analysis of religion, not its advocacy, ought to be the hallmark of its study under the arts and sciences.

3. The third specious model rests upon a superficially attractive distinction between the "theory" of religion and its "practice." According to those who make this distinction, study of religion is a consideration of the intellectual content of religious traditions. They look upon participation in religious activities as essentially separate and incidental. I find this model, which is destructive of both the academic study of religion and the genuine practice of religion, erroneous on two counts.

First, when the expression "theory of religion" is used in this context, it normally means study in the theology of one tradition or direct appropriation of the intellectual aspect primarily of one faith. But as used in the arts and sciences, "theory of religion" would more properly mean analysis of or theoretical study about religions, including their intellective aspects. Thus a phrase appropriate to the arts and sciences faculty is used in a private rather than a public fashion. Study of religion when shaped in this way misrepresents actual intentions and procedures.

Study of religion ought to be study of religious behavior, no less than of religious belief. To concentrate upon the intellectual content of religion in the name of studying the "theory of religion" is, in effect, to obscure religious behavior and, incidentally, to presuppose that religion is far more exclusively intellectual than is, in fact, the case.

My third proposition is that there ought to be nothing particularly unique about the disciplines which study religion under the auspices of a faculty of arts and sciences. Unlike the theological faculty, which takes for granted divine revelation or divinely ordained communities and traditions, the faculty of arts and sciences would be primarily interested in cultural phenomena fruitfully considered as religious, or in the multiform religious life of mankind. It is manifest that there is, broadly speaking, a class of phenomena which we conveniently label "religious" because we find resemblances and analogous roles from one culture to another. This class of phenomena, which in the West prominently includes theological reflection upon religion and religious behavior, represents the proper object for systematic and disciplined study of religion. The study of religion within the faculty of arts and sciences has no special method. Like all other cultural phenomena, religions are to be studied by those methods which seem to be appropriate. Where methods prove to be fruitful in relationship to particular ranges of subject matter, disciplines develop which quite properly become traditional. It is obvious that historical methodology has proved to be extraordinarily appropriate to the study of religious phenomena. I would judge that philosophical inquiry into both religious doctrine and religious language is equally promising. Literary analysis of religious expression would seem to claim the resources of a university or a college, and sociological and psychological studies of religious phenomena may also be worthy of support.

My final proposition is the following: Although that class of phenomena we label "religious" has nothing inherent in it which requires departmental organization for its study, the class is sufficiently coherent to warrant such organization. Departments within faculties of arts and sciences or liberal arts colleges are primarily matters of convenience, a contemporary administrative device for bringing some order out of the vitalities which abound in a university or college. Accordingly, to organize the study of religion in this way is reasonable, since it leads to methodological self-consciousness as well as to more concision regarding subject matter. All of us share the concern which President Kingman Brewster of Yale has expressed most forcefully: namely that departments may proliferate and become self-perpetuating after their usefulness has ceased. Simply as a practical matter, however, it is important that the study of religion be placed on an equal footing with, shall we say, the study of that class of phenomena we label political or those classes we understand to be essentially literary. Nevertheless, nothing ought to be done within a department of religion which could not equally be done under the auspices of another department: historical study of religion, philosophical study of religion, and so forth. By the same token, of course, this observation could be made of other departments. Take, for example, politics; in spite of the claim to uniqueness often put forward by political scientists, there is no unique discipline wherein the study of politics is carried on. Sociological, psychological, historical, and philosophical methodologies can all be concentrated upon the study of political phenomena.

I hope that these propositions will have made plausible my contention that the study of religion is at least a legitimate series of disciplines fruitfully grouped together within a faculty of arts and sciences. I certainly do not claim that the study of religion represents one discrete discipline or a discipline *sui generis*.

The fundamental point which underlies my remarks is that the study of religion must be structured by educational institutions on the basis of their legitimate traditions and their proper responsibilities. External pressures to develop according to the wishes of different constituencies must be tenaciously resisted. Without clarity regarding the kinds of issues I have discussed, we will produce only confusion out of the current attempt to foster and develop the academic study of religion.

"Objectivity" and the Study of Religion

ROBERT O. JOHANN, S. J.

The particular point which I want to consider is the pretension of the scholarly study of religion to objectivity. I agree with those who maintain that religion can be looked upon as an intellectual discipline, and that it is possible to separate the intellectual study from the practice of a creed. I take issue, however, with a statement attributed to Professor Luther Harshbarger in "A Report on an Invitational Conference on the Study of Religion in the State University" held at Indiana University in 1964. That statement comes in answer to a question which is relevant to our present considerations: "How do you answer the parents who object to you: 'You have made my child an agnostic!'?" He replies: "It is only from a pietistic conception of faith that this accusation of agnosticism has any meaning. You try to show that you are raising the level of sophistication, just as the university also does with the students' understanding of science, or political science, or literature." But the matter is much more complicated than this reply suggests, and a look at these complications can throw some light on how to structure and staff a program in religion.

The general aim of higher education is, I take it, to provide the student with the ultimate in available intellectual equipment for leading a mature and responsible life in today's world. A life will be responsible in the measure that it takes into account, in the decisions which give it its shape and style, all the factors and values and possibilities inherent in human experience. Therefore, the university exists, at least on the undergraduate level, to provide the student with the broadest possible awareness of what is involved and what is at stake in the various choices he may be called upon to make. Because this awareness is a matter of understanding, of grasping all the possible connections within experience, it is essentially intellectual in character.

These connections are fundamentally of two kinds, and the difference between the two is roughly the basis of the distinction between the sciences and the humanities. First of all, objects in our experience may be linked together in the sense that they are dynamically connected with one another. The exploration of such connections is fundamentally the concern of science. Second, the meaning of objects may be sought not simply in terms of their connections with one another, but in the bearing they have on the quality,

---

The author is a professor in the department of philosophy at Fordham University.

texture, and style of human life as a whole. It is the search for this sort of meaning that characterizes the humanities. We ignore these ulterior humanistic meanings when we deal with things "scientifically" and, as John Dewey remarks, quite properly so, "for when a sequential order of changes is determined, the final meaning in immediate enjoyments and appreciations is capable of control." However, although science takes no account of these ulterior meanings, they cannot be disregarded altogether if our understanding of anything is to be at all adequate. Only in the measure that we explore the connection between what we do and the way we deal with things, on the one hand, and what we undergo—the quality and texture of our experience as a whole—on the other, do the possibilities for control which scientific investigation opens up become humanly fruitful.

This distinction is important. Not only does it provide the basis for insisting upon humanistic studies in the university alongside strictly scientific ones, but also it illuminates the kind of objectivity that is alone possible in the realm of the humanities as contrasted with the objectivity achieved by the strict sciences. Hypotheses regarding the potential consequences that objects in our experience have with respect to one another can be tested objectively—that is, by experiments that do not involve the personal commitment, orientation, and background of the one performing the experiment. The evidence in such matters is, as it were, publicly certifiable. But interpretative hypotheses regarding the bearing of beliefs, practices, and procedures on the satisfactory quality of life as a whole are susceptible to no such objective and public tests: their verification involves the total experience and background of the one who asserts them. As Professor John Macmurray points out, "Religious doctrines (and this holds true for humanistic interpretations generally) are as problematic as scientific theories and require like them a constant revision and a continual verification in action. Their verification differs in this, that it cannot be experimental, since they are not merely pragmatic; they can be verified only by persons who are prepared to commit themselves intentionally to the way of life which they prescribe." I would prefer to put it this way: They can be understood as live options only by persons who are not already convinced, in the light of their own experience, choices, and so forth, that such a way of life would be irrational.

The relevance of all this to the scholarly study of religion in the university should be obvious. The objectivity possible in courses on the history of religions and the scientific exegesis of sacred texts is demonstrably different from the objectivity possible in a course on the philosophy of religion. In the second type of course, the professor cannot prescind from his personal orientation and the whole range of his experience, direct and indirect. The value of his interpretations will depend not merely upon his honesty and intellectual competence; it will depend on the range and depth of his personal experience to which his background and personal orientations have substantially contributed. If his experience is narrow or shallow, then his views—however acceptable academically—will be inadequate to deal with what is actually involved in the phenomena in question.

Now if we recognize along with this that students are, as a general rule, intellectually unsophisticated (in an absolute sense and relative to their sophistication in other areas of learning) about the religious traditions in which they have been born and bred, it is easy to see what can happen. A philosophic interpretation of religion, honestly and intelligently given, can raise serious doubts in a student's mind about the validity of his own tradition, with which he has himself only slight intellectual acquaintance. Moreover, there may be no one on campus who is of equal intellectual stature with the philosopher and who is, at the same time, sufficiently versed in the tradition and convinced of the sense it makes, to provide a reasonable alternative to the philosopher's position. If agnosticism results in such a situation, it is not because the student's level of sophistication has been raised generally, but because it has been raised in one area, philosophy, and neglected in another, the matter of his own religious tradition. It is not too much to say that the cards have been stacked, and quite irresponsibly, against such a student.

What conclusions are to be drawn from all this? One conclusion that I certainly do not wish to imply is that the student at a university should be simply indoctrinated in the religious beliefs which he had on entering it. This would go against what I said at the outset: that the task of the university is to give the student the widest possible awareness of all the factors, values, and *possibilities* inherent in human experience. There is no reason why any point of view that is intellectually respectable should not have a hearing. No matter how inadequate, from the standpoint of a particular religious tradition, various interpretations of the religious phenomenon may be, they are all part of human culture and can contribute substantially to the student's growth.

The point I am making is that the student's increased sophistication in other academic areas, as well as in the area of religion in general, should be matched by the opportunity for an increased sophistication in the area of his own religious tradition. Granting this point, no program of religious studies at a secular university will be fair to the student and adequate to the American scene unless it provides for explorations in depth of the great religious traditions of this country. Since it is a question of making available the best possible case—in the sense of providing a rational view, not in the sense of proselytizing—for each of these traditions (Protestant, Roman Catholic, Jewish), professors in these areas should not only be intellectually competent in them on a descriptive level; they should also be convinced adherents of the sense they make. They need not (perhaps, should not) be ministers, priests, or rabbis, but they should be persons who can bring to their task that kind of insight which, as Macmurray suggests, only a commitment to that sense can provide.

Moreover, such men should be officially and academically integrated into the university, enjoying the same privileges and subject to the same requirements as other university professors. Anything short of this is to deny them the standing and respectability required by their tasks. Although in the past such men may have been difficult to find, they are certainly less so now, and this difficulty should no longer be a factor in deciding policy. Indeed, once the universities recognize their responsibilities in this area, and seek to meet them, adequate incentive will be provided for training the large number of specialists that will be needed. That such is not yet the case is indicated by the fact that, of the ten case studies offered by Professor Michaelsen, only the program offered at Western Michigan University would seem to demonstrate an awareness of what I have been talking about.

Finally, the program which I have suggested would seem to do justice to the legitimate concerns of religious-minded parents who worry about sending their sons and daughters to secular universities. It is true that, even in such a situation as I have described, agnosticism may be the outcome. But then it would at least have the chance of being a responsible decision on the part of the student, rather than the result, as it so often is now, of the university's failure to present genuine alternatives.

Modern Poetry and Religion:
A Deepening of Perception

Barry Ulanov

It can be argued that, in the academy, religion is almost everybody's discipline. I will be making that argument, but I will not as a result be arguing against a separately constituted department of religion. I am very much concerned, however, with asserting strongly that those who teach religion need a much more sophisticated understanding of it where it touches upon the disciplines of literature and the arts, of philosophy and anthropology and sociology, of psychology, of history, of economics.

The values of religion are all the values examined in the academy, from the incendiary issues of modern genetics to judgments of the beautiful and the ugly, of right and wrong, of the cognition of truth. Any systematic or historical approach to these areas of value must touch upon religion and religious attitudes. And equally, religion as it is taught about and thought about now in American colleges and universities will sooner or later touch all these areas, and touch them with more confidence and a better equipped scholarly apparatus, I think, than it is likely to bring to the examination of the so-called spiritual values of the textures and tonalities of what used to be called holiness.

One cannot examine modern poetry—to take an area which I can speak about with some confidence—without moving boldly and probing deeply into both modern and ancient religious attitudes and religious experience. I should like to give some signifying examples of what I mean—their significations will not, I think, be obscure. If one deals with the career of T. S. Eliot, for example, one is constantly caught up in religious experience—religious experience at first mocked and shunned, then courted and finally, if the evidence of *Four Quartets* is as trustworthy as I think it is, won. But before it is attained, Eliot has touched down heavily in the thought and experience of Heraclitus, of St. John of the Cross, of Dante, of the seventeenth-century Anglican divines, of medieval cosmologists, of Lady Julian of Norwich, of the *Bhagavad-Gita*. If one makes one's investigation more searching than conversation at a cocktail party, even Eliot's *Cocktail Party*, one must examine these materials, first for oneself and then for and with one's students. To do so requires

---

The author is professor of English at Barnard College and adjunct professor of religion at Columbia University.

equipment in several disciplines, but most of all in the disciplines that take Lady Julian and John of the Cross, Dante and Lancelot Andrewes, and all those who find themselves concerned about the conflicting values of action and inaction, like Arjuna in the *Gita*, out of literature and into life. Round categorical distinctions that do not suggest the heating of the blood involved in Eliot's monologues and colloquies are next to worthless in the present-day college classroom where the *Quartets* and the poetry that led up to them are being discussed.

Suppose, for a moment, one contemplates those famous lines which conclude William Butler Yeats's sonnet, "Leda and the Swan:"

> *Being so caught up,*
> *So mastered by the brute blood of the air,*
> *Did she put on his knowledge with his power*
> *Before the indifferent beak could let her drop?*

The allusions are not obscure. Everyone knows that what was engendered by that earth-shattering "shudder in the loins" was in fact the shattering of the Greek and Trojan earth, the Trojan War itself, since Helen, the issue of the mating, was also the issue of the war and the progenitor of all the subsequent terrors including the murders of Agamemnon and Clytemnestra and Aegisthus and all the violence that attended the wanderings of Odysseus and of Aeneas. But Yeats is concerned with more than ancient history. He is asking questions that developed out of his early adventures in the occult, tutored by H. P. Blavatsky and Annie Besant and their more or less illustrious disciples and devotees. He is speculating, with his usual poetic felicity, in the realm of religious epistemology. How does one acquire knowledge of the mysteries? Is there a process, orderly or disorderly, across the experiences of sexuality, which unites the body and the spirit and the mind and which assures man of something more than a perfunctory understanding of the supernatural or the preternatural? Yeats never hesitated to examine methodologies that promised some penetration of the mysteries, no matter how obscure to his own background, no matter how remote from his own experience, no matter how close to what is generally called "crackpot." If the procedure offered the possibility of a real insight into these realms, Yeats came a-calling, and all the more vigorously and confidently after his marriage to a lady gifted, as he proudly proclaimed in *A Vision*, in trance and automatic writing.

To deal with "Leda" or the "Byzantium" poems or "A Dialogue of Self and Soul" or almost any of the fine late poems of Yeats, one must be willing to examine the language and thought of theosophy; one must be willing to sift the special tones of the translations of Yeats's personal swami, translations of the *Gita* and of Patanjali's yoga doctrines and exercises. One must be respectful about a world of experience on the fringe of the religions, but no less significant for this, either as experience or as part of the disciplinary structure of religion. If there were no other basis for respect than Yeats's own words, wouldn't that be enough? Sitting in his tower, which was not made of ivory, he sent forth his call in his "Dialogue of Self and Soul":

> *I summon to the winding ancient stair;*
> *Set all your mind upon the steep ascent,*
> *Upon the broken, crumbling battlement,*
> *Upon the breathless starlit air,*
> *Upon the star that marks the hidden pole;*
> *Fix every wandering thought upon*
> *That quarter where all thought is done:*
> *Who can distinguish darkness from the soul?*

To make sure of this, one need not share Yeats's point of view or have had his kind of experience. By analogy, one can say that to understand or to explicate Robert Graves' poetic sexuality does not require the precise experience he describes. I would not, however, quite trust a eunuch to be a useful critic of Graves.

Those who came after Yeats and Eliot did not cease to make summonings like theirs; they were not done with the spiritual combat. Edwin Muir, a poet of Eliot's generation who did not really find either his muse or his auditors until after the last world war, was also one who found his vitality as a poet in a late accretion of religious experience that resulted from a sojourn in Rome with the British Council. The crystallization of that experience for him was the imagery of the Annunciation that constantly confronted him in the votive pictures, painted or scratched or drawn across buildings, in the Roman streets. He was caught by the look exchanged between the imaged eyes of the angel Gabriel and the Virgin, *tutto tremante*, another kind of shuddering, but not unrelated to Leda's vibrating loins. The passage in his autobiography in which Muir discusses the experience is impressive. The poem he made out of it, "The Annunciation," is even more striking. It ends,

> *through the endless afternoon*
> *These neither speak nor movement make,*
> *But stare into their deepening trance*
> *As if their gaze would never break.*

What I should like to call to your attention in this poetry is the high place given popular religion, the understanding that Muir (the translator of Franz Kafka) finds in a street-corner engagement of the emotions. Perhaps it was the street corner he had in mind in these lines from the same poem:

> *Outside the window footsteps fall*
> *Into the ordinary day*

> And with the sun along the wall
> Pursue their unreturning way
> That was ordained in eternity.
> Sound's perpetual roundabout
> Rolls its numbered octaves out
> And hoarsely grinds its battered tune.

The "battered tunes" of religion have been given some entertaining outings in modern English and American poetry. John Betjeman has all but turned Westminster Abbey into a low-church chapel almost, in his variously sentimental and ironic excursions through Anglican architecture, hymnody, and the genteel theology which hovers over chancel and organ stop. His friend and first sponsor for American readers, W. H. Auden, has long since stopped singing the cracked tunes of the thirties—the Marxist madrigals and Freudian anthems, the slightly boozy blues which he gave a more acerb twist than anyone after Bessie Smith—in favor of a Kierkegaardian oratorio, a meditation of meditations, strung nervously, searchingly, in a sumptuous flow of words, on the hours of his days. Auden's tune is still battered, but it is battered now like the heart that John Donne exposed in all its nakedness to the "three-person'd God." Here, for example, is the beginning of the day, "Prime," in Auden's book of hours:

> Holy this moment, wholly in the right,
>   As, in complete obedience
> To the light's laconic outcry, next
>   As a sheet, near as a wall,
> Out there as a mountain's poise of stone,
>   The world is present, about,
> And I know that I am, here, not alone
>   But with a world, and rejoice
> Unvexed, for the will has still to claim
>   This adjacent arm as my own.

One of the triumphs of the arts in our time, as they have been touched by religion, is their eager acceptance of the world, an acceptance that is not so much a paradox as it may seem, but rather, perhaps, the final shedding of the Manichaean scab from the body of Western religion. In poetry, one thinks of Richard Wilbur's *Things of This World*, with its coupling of patristic texts and laundry hanging on a line: of ancient wisdom and the full range of experiences of ordinary life as it is lived in the modern world. In music, Karlheinz Stockhausen's electronic *Benedicite* may strike quite extraordinary sounds, but their source is a very familiar set of hums and screeches, the ones we hear all day long on the radio and television. Le Corbusier's ecclesiastical performances—the church at Ronchamp, the Dominican monastery at La Tourette—give the textures of concrete and the mathematics of random form a representation of great force in a religious setting. In all of these works, as in so much of the painting of our time that springs from religious experience or simply from the commissions of religious bodies, the central element is a fresh discourse, an unfamiliar logic—fresh to religious settings, unfamiliar to religious tradition. The discourse and the logic serve as reminders to those who work in the humanistic disciplines of how frequently in our time this communication across cultures and vocabularies has taken place under the aegis of religion. Not since the Italian Renaissance has there been so deliberate a movement from the religious world to the secular, and from the secular to the religious, less and less with any need to pretend apologetic function or to fulfill creedal purpose.

Whether out of the bonds of an inherited Christian rhetoric, as in the work of James Joyce and William Faulkner, or out of the liberation of ancient modalities newly investigated, as in the religious art of Henri Matisse, Fernand Léger, Olivier Messiaen, Arnold Schönberg, the language and the imagery and the sounds have achieved a new set of qualities; an iconology of the modern era has begun to take shape and we must deal with it in the modern academy, whether in the discipline of religion or, as is more likely, in departments of literature, music, art, and philosophy.

It is clear, I think, that the procedures of analysis that this kind of statement in the arts requires are not the consecrated modes of scholasticism. Neither verification nor justification is involved, at least not in the classroom. The value judgments—if, indeed, they are to be called judgments at all and not hypotheses or simply phenomena— are subject more to syntactical scrutiny than to examinations for fidelity to dogma, doctrine, or organized teaching of any kind. This does not mean that the analysis is necessarily superficial or that we deal here only with catalogues of experience, variously esthetic or religious. We have at our disposal a set of emblems, which signify now an experience of individual persons, now an experience of one or more communities, now a mass experience. We work with these emblems sometimes to discover intention, more frequently to find multiple possibilities of meaning, most often to develop our own consciousness of the field of human existence. We speak or write a kind of geography of the race in which all the lakes, rivers, cities, towns, hills, mountains are emblematic of the heights and the depths, the satisfactions and the frustrations of human experience.

Perhaps the most beguiling set of emblems of this kind is that presented by the modern drama. Its examination of the human condition has been conducted with great courage and a skill of almost the same dimension ever since Ibsen and Strindberg first began to expose the multiple levels of pretension, of futility, of anguish, and of hostility that they found around them. The line from this distinguished pair leads through the explorations of German expressionism and the Brechtian drama of alienation right up to the wild improbabilities of the theaters of the absurd and of cruelty, which at their best offer another considerable record of need, desire, hope, despair, and very frequently of spiritual hunger as well. In their materials, we find the same concerns, the same speculations, even some of the same solutions that we find in the philosophy and theology of our time, though stated so obliquely that we can never extract or summarize in neat tags or formulas what we find. But isn't this as it should be? Isn't this as useful in its way—this abstruseness of the modern drama, which hangs upon the abstruseness of human experience—as the deepening of the vocabulary of religious perception which has been accomplished in our day by the phenomenologists, by the philosophers of existence, by the sifters and strainers of ordinary language? It is a confusion, but a confusion less confounded, a confusion with which we can live and even, perhaps, find life more valuable as a result. I would argue, I think, that the arts and artists that have accomplished this have done a great deal to make religion almost everybody's discipline, and not merely in the academy.

Review of the Discussions

Review of the Discussions

Karl D. Hartzell

In order to give subsequent discussion as broad a basis as possible, the committee which planned the conference deliberately opened the sessions with a consideration of what function the study of religion has and with a characterization of the phenomena covered by the term "religion." As Dr. Martin, a member of the planning committee, said in his paper, much of the debate as to whether religion is a discipline, and if so, whether or how it should be pursued and taught in colleges and universities, has in the past "been vitiated by too narrow an understanding or by an insufficiently critical and informed understanding of what we are talking about when we speak of religion." Too often, those involved in such discussions "assume views based on various kinds of personal and social involvements in the religious traditions of their own culture or on the particular interests and methods of their academic field," and thus tend to distort or to prejudge the question.

The discussions at the end of each session clearly illustrated the truth of these observations. Because the participants in the conference differed so much in background and training and because the phenomena considered under the rubric of religion are so varied and complex—including, as they do, thought, attitudes, beliefs, individual and group practices, social organizations, and the impact that these have on artistic, musical, and literary expression as well as on political and economic life—it proved difficult to conduct a coherent discussion. Moreover, much time was spent on tangential questions such as the quarrel within philosophy between logical positivists and idealists, the research-teaching dichotomy, and the problem of student motivation. The failure to follow through on a particular line of thought sometimes gave the discussion a disjointed character. It was clear that when a subject was abruptly changed, the discussant had not been listening to his predecessor, but had rather been turning over in his mind a point that had been brought up some time before in the discussion and waiting for a chance to voice his opinion on it.

The quality of the discussions was a function of four factors: (1) the clarity of the initial papers (2) the extent to which the written materials that had been sent to each participant in advance had been read and digested (3) the diverse backgrounds and levels of understanding of the members of the conference, and (4) the leadership provided by those with professional interests in the field, not all of

---

The author is administrative officer of the State University of New York at Stony Brook, N. Y.

whom were speakers. In general, the papers, which were usually of high quality, established the broad orientation of each discussion section. Members of the conference sometimes had difficulty in grasping fully all the implications of what had been said even within as short a time as the fifteen minutes allotted each speaker. At no time were Dr. Michaelsen's case studies in the development of departments and curricula systematically evaluated. Although it cannot be stated with certainty just how thoroughly the participants had done their homework, it can be inferred that the materials helped to provide a background, even though few specific references to them were made.

As has been suggested, the members of the conference differed considerably in their disciplinary backgrounds. Theology and philosophy were the two disciplines best represented. A sizable number of the participants were from the social sciences and English; far fewer were from the fine arts, languages, and the natural sciences. Similarly, the range of knowledge and sophistication about religion was considerable and made for lively discussion. Most of the speakers were professionals with a synoptic and historically well-grounded knowledge of the field, and some of the participants were equally knowledgeable. Other participants approached the discussions from the standpoint of philosophy or history and could not be regarded as professionals in the field of religion. Still others had relatively limited backgrounds. The job roles of the participants also determined their interests to some extent. Obviously, the problems faced by college presidents, provosts, and deans of faculty differ from those of department chairmen or members of curriculum committees, as well as from those of interested scholars free from administrative responsibilities.

Because the discussions were unstructured apart from whatever framework was provided by the preliminary papers, they reveal what was uppermost in the minds of the conference membership—what questions were of greatest interest, what areas were of deepest personal concern. From the nature of the questions asked, one could infer a considerable range in the assumptions made and accepted. Most of the questions involved requests for clarification of what had been said or for confirmation of what the questioner understood to have been said. Much of the discussion also took the form of an exchange of views.

Although the preliminary papers did not, generally, attempt formal definitions of religion, much time was devoted to saying what religion was or was not, and by the time the discussion had progressed for four sessions, it became obvious that the word "religion" meant a number of different things to different people and that some attempt at definition might be helpful.

Although most of the members of the conference sought rational grounds for thinking about the offerings of their institutions in the field of religious studies, others seemed to have reacted negatively at some time in the past to what in their experience had passed for "religion." They appeared intent upon defending their position by defining the field of religion in such a way as to justify their continued opposition to including it in the liberal arts curriculum. To do this, they either equated religion with superstition and myth or described it as so personal and so circumscribed by emotion as to defy rational consideration. Their comments served to sharpen debate and to force a more precise explanation of what had been said by the speakers, a clearer definition of what was meant by religion and religious studies, and a careful weighing of the administrative realities as a basis for concluding that departments of religion were feasible, useful, or desirable. Considerable time was also spent debating the meaning of the term "academic discipline," and discussing whether the boundaries were set by the subject matter considered, the methodologies used, the number of active scholars in the field, or the quantity and level of scholarship produced.

On the whole, it can be said that the conference participants had ample opportunity to express themselves. In addition to the formal sessions there were informal tête-à-têtes or small group discussions during the coffee breaks, at meals, and late in the evenings, and these provided added opportunities for seeking clarification of specific points and for trying out new ideas on one's colleagues.

1. What Is the Subject Matter and the Function of the Academic Study of Religion?

The participants devoted a considerable amount of time to considering the subject matter of religion and the function of its study. The extent and complexity of the phenomena were constantly alluded to in the discussions. At no time, however, were the phenomena thoroughly classified and related logically to each other, and the failure to do this promoted confusion. Other sources of confusion were the variety and range of methodologies used in the academic study of religion and the question of how religion is related to other disciplines in the humanities.

A. *Range of Phenomena*

During the discussion of the group of phenomena called "religious," a distinction gradually developed between (1) aspects of thought such as creeds, dogmas, and beliefs; (2) social institutions such as organized churches, rituals, ceremonies and services, and professional priesthoods of the great religions; (3) the impact that the first two have on such social manifestations as architecture (cathedrals and mosques), religious art, religious music, and the political and economic activities of men motivated by religious ideas, whether charitable, hostile, or educational; and (4) the subjective concerns of the individual in his search for answers to the great questions, and as Philip Phenix put it, for "life-orientation," or "wholeness." This search for ultimate meaning was recognized as being fundamental to, or generative of, all religions throughout history. The answers which have been given to these great questions have provided what Dr. Phenix called the "animating principles of civilization."

Because religious thought and belief have been closely linked historically with cultural institutions and activities, the study of religion is an extremely complex affair. The participants had some difficulty in grasping the entire range of phenomena. Many voiced a concern that at least the core of the subject be identified in order to justify departmental status for the study of religion or to guide in the selection of courses which a small existing department might be content to offer. It was generally agreed that this core should include the study of the major religions of the East and West, especially the documents and literatures that express the thought and practice of these religions. It was also suggested that a department might concentrate on those phenomena common to all or to most religions—the distinction between sacred and profane, the role of rituals, and so forth. Dr. Glass pointed out, however, that "if the historian deals simply with the influence of religious activity upon human endeavor as illustrated in historical events, morals, and cultural developments, he runs the risk of being accused of not taking into account religion itself."

Professor Phenix's concept that religion is an attempt to achieve a comprehensive life-orientation (or, as Dr. Martin put it, a "synoptic vision") was not accepted by many of the participants, although some members of the conference pointed out that students today, like their ancestors, are still seeking answers to fundamental questions, albeit they may phrase these questions somewhat differently in the light of modern knowledge, and that professors in other branches of the humanities are called upon to provide answers to these questions.

It was generally agreed that, although this integrative function of religion was a definite part of the total spectrum of religious phenomena, it was not in itself broad enough to supply a comprehensive basis for definition.

The membership was definitely divided between those who equated religion with myth and superstition and regarded the consideration of religious phenomena as now only a matter of history, and those who recognized the persistence to the present time, among adults as well as students, of man's search for his ultimate context and the significance of his life in relation to ultimate purpose. This second group has, in the words of Dr. Michaelsen, a "feeling of great excitement" about "what is happening today in the Ecumenical Movement and in such emerging nations as Pakistan, Burma, Israel, and

India, not to mention the stirrings of religion under communism in the Soviet Union, Eastern Europe, and China." Far from being a dead subject, he felt, religion today has some very challenging frontiers.

B. Approaches to Religion

Inevitably, the complexity of religious phenomena necessitates a variety of approaches to their study. During the conference, the different methodologies used to study religion—historical, literary, philosophical, psychological, and sociological—were noted and commented upon. There was consensus about the importance of the historical approach, since the great religions evolved in time as well as in space, and about the importance of studying philosophical interpretations of the bearing of religion upon life—the impact that practices, procedures, and beliefs have on the general quality of human culture.

Some time was spent also on considering the meaning of "objectivity" in approaches to the study of literature. Professor Johann expressed doubts as to the possibility of evaluating philosophical interpretations with the same kind of objectivity as can be brought to the historical method.

Although some members of the conference made an attempt to define for religion a single methodology, most participants, including the speakers, felt that this attempt was unrealistic.

C. The Relation of Religion to the Liberal Arts

The relation of religion to the liberal arts (which were not formally defined) received considerable attention at the conference. Maintaining that religion is not a field set off by itself, Professor Phenix emphasized that universities need courses in religion and science, religion and the arts, religion and language, and religion and history. "Any historian," he said, "who examines the underpinnings of his discipline with ultimate seriousness will inevitably raise questions which are classical religious questions. . . . There is no separate methodology by which we now take a religious approach to things."

This statement served to focus attention on the relation of religion to other disciplines. Common problems and similarities of procedure were identified and the existence of what might be called an informal mutual assistance pact between religion and a number of other branches of knowledge was commented upon.

For instance, Professor Ulanov remarked that in teaching English literature, one cannot avoid questions of synoptic vision:

> All that is said about religion can equally be said about literature. Whether we like it or not, we teach confessional courses in literature: our students come to us with requests for synoptic visions, and we produce them Monday, Wednesday, and Friday, or Tuesday and Thursday, as our schedule requires. We have indulged in a grandiose language which I find somewhat repellent, but which I am stuck with, because the people I teach about, as well as the people I teach to, use this language.

In short, one can find fundamental religious questions enunciated and examined in great literature.

Provost Schlatter added,

> Everything that Professor Ulanov has said about literature could be translated into my own discipline, history, where the problems of interpretation and understanding come up all the time. Unless one has some access to religious knowledge, one cannot really deal with these problems.

The interdependence of religion and other liberal arts was again illustrated by Professor Ulanov:

> I think it is important that my colleagues in English and Drama have enough awareness of and respect for the religious foundation of the materials they deal with that they take time to examine that foundation and even to go to specialists simply to learn to ask questions. It is ridiculous to deal with Yeats's kind of theosophy with contempt. It is unfortunate perhaps from many points of view that he was a theosophist. But it is not unfortunate from the point of view of great verse.

Professor Martin put it this way:

> The subject matter is vast enough to engage us all. It is relevant to all of our disciplines, to some more obviously than to others, perhaps. But most of us will be appropriately engaged, when we ask about the religious from the standpoint of whatever discipline we are involved in. Conversely, a professor in a department of religion who is interested in investigating ritualistic phenomena in various religious traditions should be anthropologically informed. He might even want a cultural anthropologist who was interested in religion to undertake this investigation. It is not a matter of either-or, but of how the task may best be done in a particular institution at a particular time.

The need for mutual assistance is perhaps best summarized by Professor Welch:

> It occurs to me that what those in departments of religion and those in other liberal arts fields really need to do is to keep each other honest. As Mr. Wilson suggested at one point, it may be that everything that is done in a department of religion could be done elsewhere in the university. Were it done right, this might be satisfactory. As a matter of empirical fact, it is *not* done satisfactorily.
>
> One of the practical aspects of having a department or a specialized program in religion is that it keeps professors in other disciplines honest. If every person in literature, for example, were able to treat religious matters with the sophistication of Barry Ulanov, then there would be no problem, but very often, professors fail to recognize what should be dealt with. Correlatively, it is of the very greatest importance that the historian in *his* discipline should keep the man who is dealing with the history of Western religions honest, that the Orientalist should keep the man who is dealing with Far Eastern religions honest. We are not talking here at all about opposition, but about mutual support and complementary kinds of programs.

Professor Ulanov thought that specialists in religion are always available and that "it is the scholarly obligation of people teaching outside religion to find those experts."

2. What Is the Purpose of Teaching Religion?

Although this topic was not originally on the agenda of the conference, it could not be avoided, since the needs and development of the student are integral to the context of the entire concept of liberal education. The basic argument for teaching religion is no different from the argument for teaching any other aspect of human culture. As Professor Welch stated in his paper, "one of the functions of a college or university is to provide opportunity for the disciplined, sustained, critical, free study of *all* the domains of human experience. . . . Religion is such a domain." Because a liberal education is concerned broadly with human culture, past and present, and because religion is a major component of culture, students, if they are to be liberally educated, must know something about religion if they are to understand their own and other societies. Professor Wekerle summarizes this point of view:

> The argument for the study of religion is precisely to make the student aware—logically, historically, and personally—of the phenomenon of religion in human life. To understand the Far East, for instance, one simply cannot strike religion from the map of knowledge. And to understand what is going on in the contemporary period, one must understand the history of Christianity.

Members of the conference were convinced that, in addition to presenting religion as part of the human culture and one of the liberal arts, an equally important purpose in the teaching of religion has to do with the effect of this study upon the student himself. Professor Johann argued that a student should have a chance to raise his level of sophistication in the area of his own religious tradition as well as in other areas; he should not be condemned to retain the religious orientation of his childhood, a case of arrested development by fiat. Religion as an area of inquiry, it was argued, should be kept alive in the mind of the student; he should be made aware, as part of his liberal education, of the phenomena in this field just as he should be of the phenomena of the arts or literature or philosophy.

Although, as Professor Wilson put it in the discussion, "One does not define a discipline in terms of human needs," (which is probably the principal reason why chaplains and deans of students were not invited to the conference), many of the speakers and discussants called attention to the deep concern that students have for answers to the great questions, emphasized the importance of meeting the needs of students, and stressed the role of religion in the formation of character and in intellectual and personal growth. Dr. Glass, Dr. McEwen, Dr. Nelson, and Dr. Ulanov were especially explicit on this point. In effect, they were saying that the age-old religious questions which man has faced and which he faces still, are the same ones that students begin to be aware of when they get to college.

The discussion repeatedly dodged the two horns of the teaching dilemma: the Scylla of indoctrination or evangelism and the Charybdis of objectivity carried to such an extreme as to leave the mind of the student untouched. Although the speakers and many of the participants explicitly denied that the academic study of religion should be in any sense evangelistic, some members of the conference claimed that, because of religion's emotional content, most teachers are unable to teach it without indoctrinating their students.

In discussing what effect the teaching of religion should have upon the student, some participants touched on what they considered to be the desired effect of all liberal arts courses on the outlook and habits of mind of students. As Dean Hakim of Seton Hall put it,

> I wonder if we are not in danger of concerning ourselves so much with objectivity as defined by Dr. Welch that we lose sight of religion entirely. There is a fear of evangelizing, of having the student accept the teacher's presentation and his faith uncritically. Surely there is a middle course; one can avoid the extreme of evangelizing and at the same time avoid the other extreme of finishing an entire course without affecting the student's habit of mind at all. In a course in the history of philosophy, one attempts to develop in the student what might be called a true philosophical habit of mind, one that grows out of his own personal experience, his response to reality as he now sees it. Shouldn't something like this be the aspiration of the teacher of religion: to induce in the student a religious habit of mind that proceeds from his personal experience. . . . There is something in religion, more than in other subject areas, that requires a personal response.

Dr. Welch's rejoinder was,

> Probably those of us at certain kinds of institutions bend over backwards to be objective, more than our colleagues in a great many other disciplines do. Maybe we ought to be rather proud of ourselves. Clearly, it is not permissible to bind the conscience of the student. However, this does not rule out the possibility of the teacher's attempting to articulate—fully and clearly and vigorously—his own understanding of things or that of the religious community to which he belongs. Although he should not deliberately set out to persuade the student to his position, this may be the unintentional result.

Professor Johann added to this:

> If the student leaves a course in the study of religion without having understood that religious matters are important and without developing some sympathy for the problems involved, some kind of engagement with them, even though it be a negative engagement, a reaction against religion, then the professor has failed.

Extensive though the interest was in meeting the needs of students—one dean of the faculty stated he thought "we would all agree that is our primary responsibility"—a number of speakers pointed out that they did not mean by the term "religion," "the care of souls" nor "catechetical instruction in the faith," and that they did not consider the study of religion to include the "counseling of students." But some participants who were fundamentally opposed to the study of religion in a university persisted in maintaining that these were the major purposes served by any courses in religion.

Perhaps the best summary of the conflicting points of view which were expressed concerning the purpose of the teaching of religion was given by Walter Watson of Stony Brook:

> There is a kind of opposition or conflict between two interests that is not sufficiently dealt with in terms of "keeping each other honest." On the one hand, there is the interest of the scholar that the academic study of religion not be corrupted by a concern with the salvation of souls or the needs of students. On the other hand, there is the interest expressed by Father Johann and others that the teaching of religion be in touch with the problems that the student feels, that it not be divorced from the genuine religious problems that he confronts.
>
> I would like to suggest that these two interests are not necessarily in opposition. It seems to me quite possible to have an intellectual discipline with a practical end. There are many such disciplines. Ethics is one example. In teaching ethics, there are two wrong extremes. One is to tell people what to do, how to act. We do not want to do that. On the other hand, it is a mistake to teach ethics as a purely theoretical discipline, a linguistic analysis of the meaning of "good" and "right," without a consideration of their bearing on conduct. It is possible to take an intermediate position, to teach argument, intellectual structure, or discipline, but to relate these to conduct and action. The same is true in criticism and the arts. You can teach an intellectual structure that will eventuate in an appreciation of what the art is. I think something analogous is possible in the case of religion. You do not have to separate the rigorous intellectual content from an ultimate practical justification.

3. What Is an Academic Discipline and Is Religion Such a Discipline?

Although the term "discipline" was never clearly defined, certain characteristics were noted or implied from time to time, and by the end of the conference, a rough description could be given. Apparently, an academic discipline consists of what scholars are engaged in studying or doing and of the assembled records of what scholars have done in the past. Disciplines do not come into being merely because they ought to exist. They are the result of the association of many minds working in the same area of inquiry, and consequently they are a function of systematic interest and common effort.

Disciplines arose originally in answer to somebody's intellectual curiosity, somebody's desire to know. At first, the questions asked were simple and untutored, but they grew more and more sophisticated as they came to be based on an over-expanding knowledge and as both questions and answers could be checked and double-checked by others in the same field of research. It was pointed out too that a discipline may have subfields. As Dr. Martin said, "The phenomena tend to set the scale."

The critical size for a corps of scholars is anybody's guess. However, the number of scholars must apparently be large enough to develop what Dr. Nelson referred to as "a recognized language" and to employ recognized methods. Also, the group of scholars and the systematic character and scope of their activities must be acknowledged and respected by members of other academic disciplines. Such informal recognition constitutes a kind of necessary academic imprimatur.

The frequent opposition to accepting religion as a distinct discipline was expressed by a number of participants. As Provost Schlatter pointed out, resistance can be expected from those in other disciplines and other departments, purely on the basis of competition for funds, space, and equipment. Professor O'Dea mentioned that at Columbia, the Department of Sociology protested the establishment of a department of religion on the ground that religion lacked a methodology. Although Professor Nelson and Professor Ulanov emphasized that the university is responsible for supporting the scholarly study of religion, neither was willing to accept the implied equating of such activity with Professor Michaelsen's assumption in *The Scholarly Study of Religion* that religion is a separate and distinct discipline.

The frequent questions about methodologies seemed to divide themselves into two categories. Does every discipline have its own unique methodology? Does religion have, or must it have, a single methodology in order to be considered a discipline? In response to the question of how important methodological coherence or intrinsic logic is to the existence and development of a department, Dr. Schlatter said, "It seems to me one would have a hard time defending the position that existing departments all have clear, concise, definable methodologies."

The issue of methodologies provoked some very interesting comments. Mr. Sasscer said,

> I have the feeling that the methodology which is prominent in a great number of fields—in English literature, and in sociology, for instance—is the historical approach. And, let's face it, as long as people are willing to study the history of something and to use the historical method accompanied by appropriate textual criticism—the historical-critical method, if you want to call it that—they are fairly happy.

However, Professor Nelson pointed out that,

> One of the reasons that everyone is ready to adopt a so-called historical-critical method is that history is a departmental study in which, by general agreement of historians, anyone is free to do pretty much as he likes. No subject matter is more lax in that regard.

He added that many historians are teaching social science and that their methods of explanation were social-scientific; he also charged that, in many institutions, the history of literature is being taught in such a way that it no longer qualifies as one of the humanities.

Dr. Hyman indicated that he, too, was troubled by the methodological issue, which seemed to be more complex than Mr. Sasscer's explanation would imply. He cited as an example the teaching of the Bible:

> As I studied it at the university, and as it is generally taught, the historical-literary approach is taken, with perhaps a little archeology thrown in. Now it seems to me that, as one approach, this is quite justified. It is one way in which the Bible is studied in our society. But let us take the next step. Suppose the student is interested in the patristic or rabbinic or Reformation exegesis of the Bible. (I assume that these disciplines have their own methodologies.) To say at this point, "Well, literary or historical study is all right, but patristic or rabbinic studies are not all right," seems to me unjustified. Historically speaking, there have been many different approaches to the Bible and to other aspects of religious literature and religious phenomena, and we should keep that diversity in mind.

Some participants in the conference maintained that a discipline need not have a singular methodology: it may have one or it may have many, depending on the complexity of the phenomena to be studied.

As Professor Wilson said in his paper, "The study of religion within the faculty of arts and sciences has no special method. Like all other cultural phenomena, religions are to be studied by those methods which seem to be appropriate."

Nevertheless, some members of the conference felt that most disciplines have a unique methodology, that they can therefore be defined in terms of their methodologies, and that without a unique methodology there can be no discipline. Thus they argued that religion is not a discipline and should not be included in the curriculum. Dr. Stewart Gordon noted:

> It has not been sufficiently emphasized here that many people outside of this conference regard the subject matter of religion as little more than superstition and the study of religion as a relic of the Middle Ages. People holding such views are fairly common in the academic world, and their opposition, perhaps more than anything else, prevents the establishment of departments of religion.

The apparent lack of a unique methodology was also stressed by Professor Watson, who said that he hoped to get from the conference some sense of what religion would be as a discipline. Although he could grasp that religion has a distinct subject matter, he equated the many differences of approach with differences of disciplines. "You have a whole lot of other disciplines to investigate a common subject matter, but no discipline of religion itself."

Later on, however, he took a somewhat different approach:

> With respect to the problem of departmentalization, we tend to talk as if the alternatives were either a discipline proper to the subject or a subject matter—some phenomena—to which you can apply the various other disciplines. I think that this is in a way a mistake, because what in fact happens is that religion utilizes all the other disciplines from the standpoint of its own requirements. Other disciplines do this too. For

example, in the study of English literature, which I think is a discipline, one brings in knowledge acquired in various other fields. What I think Father Johann proposed was a way in which religion itself could become architectonic with respect to other disciplines and thus become the basis of a department.

In his paper, Professor Martin expressed the all-embracing character of the subject in somewhat similar terms:

> The phenomena tend to set the scale. . . . The problem of the methodologies and the styles involved, given the broadly human character of the phenomena, makes a consideration of the study of religion as an academic discipline a microcosm of the macroscopic concerns that the higher learning has with all things human.

The complexity of the subject matter of religion seems to require numerous approaches and a variety of methodologies. In the final analysis, the insistence that religion must have its own unique methodology before it can be considered a discipline and thus granted departmental status appears to be unrealistic and was not generally accepted by members of the conference.

A discipline represents the institutionalization of a certain set of questions and answers and the existence of a group of people who are concerned with studying them. At what point are the questions and answers sufficiently agreed upon and the group of scholars sufficiently large to dignify such study by the label "discipline?" Naturally those working in the field will come to the conclusion that a discipline exists sooner than those outside the field, because they themselves take such study seriously and because they know the other scholars involved in such study. Those outside may not sense the importance, or understand the nature, of either the questions or the answers, and thus may fail to take the subject and its impact on culture seriously.

4. How Should Religion Be Taught?

Objectivity, sympathetic understanding, and scholarship were three key terms in the discussions of how religion should be taught.

As might be expected, there was considerable debate about what is meant by "objectivity" in dealing with religious subject matter. In his paper, Professor Welch maintained that "objectivity involves appropriateness to the object being studied" and that this holds true for philosophy, literature, and history as well as for religion. The area of experience treated in the study of religion should, however, be "available to public scrutiny"; the phenomena must be "in the public domain."

It was also pointed out that the student, in dealing with apparent conflicts between his own childhood faith and the knowledge he acquires in the university, must regard religion as an area to be approached in a spirit of free and open inquiry.

Several members of the conference insisted that, to lay claim to objectivity, a department of religion need not necessarily represent all the major religious positions or teach by the "confessional" principle. No department should be regarded as a museum or a zoo, responsible for exhibiting all species of believers. Teachers should, however, be sufficiently sympathetic with the major religious traditions to believe that they make sense in themselves.

Early in the conference, objective phenomena—the concrete manifestations of religion such as churches, cloisters, seminaries, and parsonages, and the organizational aspects such as sects, clergy, laity, services, and creed—were distinguished from subjective interpretations of these phenomena.

Professor Johann elaborated on this point:

> An easy sort of distinction can be made between the study of religion phenomenologically—the history of religion, the exegesis of certain texts, etc., where one can have a sort of scientific objectivity—and interpretation, where you do not have the same possibility of verification or confirmation. The interpretation is there—subjective factors enter in, and we cannot rule out these aspects when we study religion at the university level.

That in some instances objectivity was simply a cloak for ignorance, was noted by Professor Adelson:

> One aspect that we have tended to ignore, is the insipid, antiseptic quality of the instruction that is given in religion by professors of history, sociology, and psychology. There is nothing more pointless than listening to a historian whose knowledge of theology, and of the fine points of dogma is limited discuss the matter of church history in the Middle Ages. If we want to teach students a discipline, we must teach it at the university or college level. To reduce it in any way is to give them less than their fair share. That, I think, is the greatest argument for a department of religion made up of true scholars. They must be people who can discuss at the appropriate level, people who can treat the problems as problems.

Several speakers made the point that "objectivity," in a strictly scientific sense, was probably a misleading term and that what is required is sympathetic understanding. Professor Moran expressed it as follows:

> I think in order to understand religious thinkers today, one has to get inside the context to see what they are doing. The specialist must accept the religious thinker on his own terms. The faculty of a department of religion must understand thoroughly the whole context in which a religious thinker worked.

Professor Johann used the analogy of philosophy to illustrate the importance of sympathetic understanding:

> I would hate to see metaphysical questions being handled by a person who is convinced that all such questions are meaningless. If that is his conviction, he cannot give any insight into the metaphysical tradition. Similarly, I would not want to see the analytic tradition exposed to a convinced metaphysician who believes that the analytic method, though a useful tool, is basically trivial in content. It seems to me that the teacher should feel that,

basically, the approach makes sense. If he decides a priori that it makes no sense, he is not going to be able to give an understanding of it. The person who teaches about a religious tradition need not be formally affiliated with it, but he should be a convinced adherent of the sense it makes.

Commenting on this view, Dr. Schlatter said,

> It seems to me that Professor Johann is really not talking about religion; he is talking about the difference between a scholar and a pedant. A scholar is a man who thinks that his field or subject is important, that it has a significant bearing on life. This conviction is necessary in other fields besides religion. The historian who thinks that the Middle Ages are the bunk should not be a medieval historian. He has to think that the way the people lived in the Middle Ages is an important phenomenon, that they are interesting as human beings.

Dr. Gross made a similar point:

> Professor Johann is actually talking about the way that any course in the university ought to be taught. The teacher should try to find the sense in his subject matter, to get a feel for it, not to condemn it. It is a question of the quality not just of a department or course but of the whole university.

The plea for scholarship was forcefully made by many participants. Essentially three points were emphasized: (1) the field of religion should be extended through scholarly research, (2) religion should be taught by men who are themselves scholars in the field, and (3) religious subject matter should be treated with respect and scholarly understanding by those who approach it from the standpoint of other disciplines.

It was acknowledged readily enough that in some departments the level of undergraduate teaching is too generalized to be academically respectable. This is not the case, however, in the major universities which have a corps of scholars—"a community of reflective minds constantly checking and rechecking each other."

Perhaps the most succinct statement about the need for a corps of scholars was made by Professor O'Dea in relation to sociology:

> What happens in most sociology departments is that one learns technique very well, but one does not get very much substance. One learns theory very well too, but one does not penetrate with any depth into a substantive area. If that is going to happen in the sociology of religion, then there is going to have to be a department of religion. There is going to have to be some kind of conversation between people like myself who are studying the sociology of religion and people who are doing substantive and phenomenological views of religion from their particular disciplinary perspectives.

Another argument for having a group of competent scholars with broad perspective on the field of religion as an area of inquiry was that this arrangement would make for less difficulty with students and parents. Underlying this discussion was the recognition that the religious beliefs of students entering the university are almost bound to come into conflict at some point or other with modern knowledge, and that it is inevitable that such an intellectual conflict will lead the student to serious questioning and much searching of heart. In

Dr. Glass's view, the university has a real responsibility for dealing with this situation whether the student is taking a course in religion or a course in biology or literature.

Considerable attention was given to the function of the courses in other disciplines which deal with religious subject matter. Because religious thought and action pervade large segments of every culture, inevitably religious phenomena should be approached in many ways and considered by various disciplines. Some participants felt that, because of its sacredness, religion should be considered only peripherally in departments other than religion. Others maintained that it is essential that scholars in other disciplines have a thorough and accurate perspective of religious phenomena. Professor Ulanov suggested, "The man who teaches drama or the novel must learn whatever religion is involved, at least enough so that he deals with it with something like scholarly understanding." Dr. Martin agreed, but added that "Unless there is some focus, unless there is some domain and some structure which has as its particular mandate the calling attention to, the investigation of, the examination of, the religious in all of its areas, the task is likely not to get done."

Dr. Michaelsen illustrated the inadequacy of some scholars' view of religion:

> There is a man in the English Department who teaches a course called "The Bible as Literature." Now this kind of course has always bothered me. This man begins by bringing in a copy of the Bible and throwing it on the floor and stamping on it to illustrate something about his approach. We had W. F. Albright, a distinguished English archeologist, on our staff for a while and we tried to establish some contact between him and the people in the English Department who offer this course. Most of them could not have cared less about Albright.

To this, Professor O'Dea responded,

> I have no use for courses in the Bible as English literature, or as Latin literature, or as Hebrew literature, but I am concerned about literature which has biblical sources. It is being taught by people who have this Bible-stamping approach, who would rather throw it on the floor and jump on it than to make use of the scholarship which should inform their examination of George Herbert's or of Henry Vaughan's use of scriptural sources. Until we demand that kind of scholarship of those who teach where religion touches on their discipline, we are going to get a very sloppy performance. Most of my colleagues assume that where their studies involve religion, any encyclopedia, any dictionary, any kind of generalized approach to this information will do. And if one calls this into serious question, one gets into a very nasty argument indeed. This attitude seems incredible, it seems jejune, it seems left over from the last century, but it is still with us.

Objectivity, sympathetic understanding, and scholarship—all three were emphasized in the discussion. Talking about the approach to popular religions, Professor Ulanov made the point that these three criteria are not incompatible:

> It seems to me that in a department of religion, or in courses on religion, popular religious ideas must be taken up with scholarly detachment and with

interest too. I see no contradiction; they go together. You can't really have the detachment without the interest. That is the paradoxical nature, I think, of the academic performance. Until we have this respect for *every* kind of religious experience, we will be doing a very bad teaching job indeed. Popular religions are as real as revolutions, and they sometimes involve many more people. They are the phenomena of our existence, and if we don't deal with them, what sort of academy do we have?

5. Who Should Teach and Where Should They Be Trained?

The plea for scholarship and objectivity can be answered only if professional scholars trained as students of religion in the broadest meaning of the term are available. It was generally agreed that scholars properly trained in the field of religious studies are in short supply and that to be properly qualified, they must have the same general kind of undergraduate and graduate education as those concentrating in any discipline. Moreover, they must be distinguished, as they are now, from the practicing clergy or the members of a faculty of theology.

The participants felt that regardless of the teacher's religious background, the quality of his scholarship would alone entitle him to the respect of his colleagues. Whatever his personal commitment to this or that tradition, he must consider his field, in the phrase of Professor Ulanov, "with scholarly detachment and interest." Dean McEwen put it this way:

> Students come to college with certain religious beliefs and religious experiences. Frequently, these conflict with other ideas that they receive in their college experience. It requires the type of teacher who has a commitment to inquiry—whether or not he is a participant in a particular religion or not—and sufficient epistomological sophistication to point out that a view which the student has received from his church training may be assumed by the priest or rabbi or clergyman holding that view to be absolutely true, but that the student need not hold it dogmatically. Like all other ideas, it may be regarded with an attitude of inquiry.

The essential problem of producing enough qualified scholars was summarized by Professor Martin:

> We are dealing with a very central issue with respect to the question that has been consistently raised, "Where does one find a properly qualified scholar?" We tend to get into a vicious circle here. We say there are not enough properly qualified scholars, so we do not do what we ought to be doing in undergraduate and graduate departments. If we do not *begin* to do something about it, we will never produce properly qualified scholars.

He pointed out that, too frequently, the department of religion has been asked to do "all things for all men" and that the typical undergraduate teacher of religion is expected "to teach all sorts of things across the board." It is increasingly recognized, however, that there are certain minimal data which people in the field should be acquainted with and which should be provided in any kind of basic core curriculum. Martin went on to say,

> We have got to get out of the straightjacket of having religious generalists doing all the jobs. We increasingly need to develop specialized scholars. If we do think that the subject matter is important and appropriate scholarship is demanded, we have got to begin, and we can't wait to begin at the graduate level.

Martin added, however, that the graduate schools are now beginning to get students with sounder preparation:

> We recognize that there is a general field of knowledge, and that the general field is relevant to various aspects of the liberal arts discipline; and we develop our small departments recognizing the need for both general knowledge and specialization. Only when we have both together can we really get ahead with the development of the field.

In connection with this problem of training, attention was called to the distinctions that can be made between (1) a theological faculty, where inquiry is carried on within the context and in the service of a community of faith, (2) a school of religion or a seminary which prepares persons for the priesthood or ministry, and (3) a graduate school with a department of religion that may deal with theology as one of the aspects of religious life.

6. How Should the Teaching of Religion Be Organized?

At the conference the tides of argument and counterargument, statement and counterstatement, that swirled around the question of how the teaching of religion should be organized at the university level repeated most of the arguments for and against departmental status that have been advanced in years past. The struggle of the study of religion to achieve departmental status tends to recapitulate the past struggles of other disciplines to be included in the liberal arts curriculum.

A. *Arguments Against Departmental Organization*

The argument against establishing a department of religion rests on five major points: (1) the indeterminate or complex character of the field, (2) the shortage of scholars, (3) the lack of any inherent reason for organizing the field—or any field, for that matter—as a department, (4) the weaknesses of departmental organization, and (5) the judgment that courses in other departments, taken together, are adequate for a satisfactory interdisciplinary program. One negative argument goes this way: Scholars in the field of religion are in short supply. Too many existing religion departments are staffed by ministers who lack scholarly training and who usually act as representatives of the "pan-Protestant Establishment." Hence, as a practical matter, a university should hold off on the establishment of a department, lest it find itself doing a substandard job.

Another negative argument is that, though systematic study and genuine scholarship may exist in the field of religion, this does not necessarily make religion a discipline (characteristics unspecified), and even if it were a discipline, there is no inherent reason that it should be organized as a department at the university level. The reluctance of some members of the conference to accept the study of religion as being entitled to departmental status reflects the attitude of academicians everywhere, an attitude that springs principally from an awareness of the weaknesses inherent in the departmental structure generally.

This negative and seemingly paradoxical position is exemplified in the statement made by Professor Ulanov during one of the discussions:

> I believe the American university, never so much as now, has the profound responsibility of encouraging the scholarly study of religion by just about everybody—all professors. But it does not necessarily follow that there has to be a given organization, a given department.

B. Arguments in Favor of Departmental Organization

In his paper, Professor Wilson pointed out that, though religious phenomena have nothing inherent in them that demands that they be treated in a separate department, they are sufficiently coherent to warrant such treatment. For sheerly practical reasons, he says, "it is important that the study of religion be placed on an equal footing with, shall we say, the study of that class of phenomena we label political or those classes we understand to be essentially literary."

Granting these practicalities, there are nonetheless certain administrative difficulties connected with establishing a department of religion. Dr. Schlatter points out that to do so,

> You have to have a chairman and a chairman has to be paid a little more than other people. Then you have to have a secretary, then you have to have a telephone, then you have to have space. And these are the practical difficulties involved in the establishing of a department.

Although the alternative was implied, no explicit proposals for establishing an interdisciplinary program in religion were made. The closest approach to such a proposal was the statement that such courses as "the sociology of religion," the "psychology of religion," the "philosophy of religion" and the Bible as literature" would suffice to cover the field at the college level.

As Mr. Sasscer put it, however, "If you don't have a department, you are dead in a lot of contemporary institutions; you cannot live in the interstices of the other departments." Dr. Schlatter elaborated on this point:

> The question has been raised as to why you cannot teach religion in another department. The fact is that you cannot. I have tried it. You go into a psychology department and you say, "Look, if I give you a new teaching position, will you add a psychologist of religion?" They say, "Well, sure, but we would rather have a rat man." And then you go to a sociology department, and they have other fields that are more interesting to them. In short, other departments are just not interested in dealing with religion, so the teaching simply does not get done.

Dr. Michaelsen made a similar comment:

> I personally think there is more evidence of seriousness if you decide to establish a separate department. This seems to be the way that things get done in the university. From what I have seen of interdepartmental programs, such as the one at Michigan, they just don't get off the ground. There is nobody minding the store.

One of the best arguments for assembling a core of scholars was expressed by Dr. Wekerle:

> It seems to me that we need a group of scholars—whether in a religion department, a philosophy department, or an interdepartmental program—whose responsibility it is to bring together what is now fragmented and dissipated over the curriculum. Until we have such a group, it will not be possible to do justice to religious phenomena or to the education of students.

The positive argument may be summarized as follows: If religion is a sufficiently coherent class of phenomena, if those who study it are of high scholarly standing and accomplishment, and if the reasons for teaching religion are cogent and compelling, then as a practical matter, the best way to insure that this field receives the necessary support in a university is to make it a department. Only then can a single individual who serves as chairman be held responsible for program, selection of personnel and preparation of the budget. Even if departments are acknowledged to have the weaknesses implied in the words "compartmentalization of knowledge," and even if they run the dangers of resistance from other departments, they obviously have administrative value in the modern university and probably academic survival value as well. Anything short of departmental structure is not likely to achieve the goal of teaching students about religion.

C. Organization Within a Department

Toward the end of the fourth period of discussion, the conference shifted its attention to the question of how best to implement a program of religion *within* a department. Dr. Michaelsen re-emphasized the primacy of scholarship and the importance of having a balanced department:

> For a number of years, I worked in an institution—the University of Iowa—where this balance was built in. There, it was provided from the very beginning that there would be a Jew, a Catholic, and a Protestant on the faculty. As dean of the school of religion I came to have real problems with this. It seemed to me that this was going at it backwards. The standard of scholarship, not the teacher's religious affiliation, should be the primary consideration.
>
> Nonetheless, as an operational or administrative matter, I would be upset with a department of religion or religious studies which had a faculty of six to eight, all of whom were liberal Protestants in their orientation, whatever their scholarly interests and competences. Such a department would lack color.

In response to a request that he consider the question of implementation in the light of his *Case Studies* and his own experiences in two state universities, Dr. Michaelsen made the following observations:

> I don't really feel that there is some model every university has to follow. I would be appalled if the University of California system were suddenly to impose from the top a model for a department of religion on all the campuses. . . . The University of Illinois has a committee which is trying to develop an interdepartmental program but does not plan to start a department. This is their context. This is the decision they made. They can't cover the waterfront.

Dr. Michaelsen also mentioned that, realistically, the future of a department of religion depends not only upon the quality of the scholars who work in it, but also upon the kind of enrollments that are attained in the courses. "Although we aren't exactly running a popularity contest, we must be very careful to appoint men who are first-rate teachers as well as first-rate scholars, and that is not easy. In general, it is easier to tell if a man has real promise as a scholar than to tell if he has real promise as a teacher."

7. The Extent of Consensus

It is always difficult to estimate the degree of unanimity that exists among members of any group. However, an examination of the transcript of the discussions gives some hints on this matter.

There was probably greater consensus than appeared on the surface. Those who opposed the study of religion as a serious subject of inquiry did so on fundamental grounds. They felt that religion is nothing but myth, an anachronism not to be taken seriously. Frequently, their hostility stemmed from the mistaken impression that answers to religious questions conceived during the childhood of the race or during their own childhood constituted the sum total of religious thought; they lacked a sophisticated understanding of religious questions and answers as they are formulated in the light of modern knowledge. They were, however, given full opportunity to express their views, and they proved to be as outspoken as were those basically in favor of the academic study of religion. Quite a number of people in this second group concentrated on understanding what was being said and formulating their own position; consequently they were not especially vocal.

That religious phenomena are broad and varied was generally acknowledged to be fact, but there was some question as to whether, and more particularly as to how, these phenomena should be studied at the college and university level. Although the feeling was by no means unanimous, it was generally held that some program for the study of religion should be inaugurated. In fact, probably most of the participants came from institutions in which some work in religion was offered, although not necessarily by a department of religion.

Everyone agreed that, if a program of religion were to be inaugurated, the scholarly standing and accomplishments of the people selected to teach it, rather than their doctrinal affiliations, were all-important considerations. Although commitment to a particular religious tradition was not thought to be essential to the study and teaching of that tradition, many participants expressed the sentiment that such a commitment usually helps because it provides serious orientation and greater insight. Again and again, the sheer necessity of taking the subject matter seriously was emphasized.

No very precise definition of an academic discipline was given. The term was used loosely, almost interchangeably with "field" or "area," except that it also connoted *how* the field or area was studied. The characteristics of the subject matter determine the subfields within a discipline and set the requirements for the methodologies to be used. It was generally, although not unanimously, agreed that a discipline is not necessarily defined in terms of a particular methodology nor by the methodologies used by scholars from other disciplines who are working in the field of religion.

Professor Hyman pointed out quite correctly that little attention had been paid to evaluating the materials sent to each participant:

> We could very well have taken, for example, Professor Michaelsen's book, his studies of religion and curricula in different universities, and evaluated these curricula. We haven't done this, and I think this omission is rather significant. As I see it, our concerns were more theoretical than practical. This would suggest that the theoretical study of the area of religion merits clarification before one can speak of its practical implementation. I myself am not unhappy about this result of our conference.

Nevertheless, it was made clear that, as a matter of practical fact, programs of studies in religion have been established, and will probably continue to be established, in many ways. Usually, in the past they have grown out of the labors of one man or of a committee which gained the respect and acceptance of the faculty as a whole because of the standing and reputation of the people involved and because of the students' acceptance of the curricular offerings. The context of each university was different, "contingent upon historical circumstances"; there was no standard commercial model to be purchased in the open market. It was also clear that the establishment of a core of offerings, whether designated as an interdisciplinary program or as a departmental program, does not necessarily mean that all courses which have the study of religious phenomena as their purpose will be absorbed in that core of offerings. In fact, cross-listing and the inclusion of courses from other departments among those required for majors in the program or department are common.

As might have been anticipated, the notion that the study of religion should be established as a separate department was most vociferously opposed, though many participants said that, in view of the prevailingly departmental character of the university administrative structure, the study of religion would be slighted unless it were carried out under the auspices of a department. To leave such studies to the discretion of other departments would mean that religious phenomena would not receive adequate scholarly attention.

8. What Did the Conference Accomplish?

Although the discussions may not have effected any remarkable changes in the attitudes or intellectual positions of the participants, undoubtedly some came away with altered viewpoints. In general, it is safe to conclude that participation in the conference helped to raise the level of sophistication about certain key points under discussion. Of those members of the conference who came in search of answers to specific questions about content, method, or procedure, some undoubtedly profited in a concrete way by attendance. Undoubtedly, being exposed to scholars who have won a national reputation in the field of religion and who represent the three major religious traditions in America was a useful experience for all the members of the conference.

One particularly cogent summary of the conference was given by Professor Arthur Hyman of Yeshiva University. Because of its lucidity and comprehensiveness, it is quoted at length.

> In our discussion at this conference, we quickly ruled out two approaches to the study of religion: the approach appropriate to a school of theology and what was called the evangelical or confessional approach. Various speakers emphasized that the subject matter of religion must be in the public domain, that religion as an academic discipline must have the same standards as any other academic discipline, and that the teacher of religion must possess high professional competence. There seemed to be consensus on these points.
>
> As I listened to the discussion, however, I discerned certain "areas of uneasiness"—that is, areas about which no ready consensus emerged. There seem to me to be six such areas.
>
> The first involves the fundamental question of whether we should encourage the teaching of religion as an academic discipline in colleges and universities, particularly in those that are supported by public funds. Occasionally a dissenting voice was heard, but in most of our deliberations we seemed to share the assumption that it is desirable to further such studies. But in reflecting on the conference, I am no longer sure that the agreement is as widespread as it appeared to be. Perhaps we were too polite to one another and did not air sufficiently our differences on this point.
>
> The next two areas of uneasiness may be considered together: Does religion have an indigenous subject matter? Does it have a distinct methodology? I must confess that before I came to the conference, my views about these two questions were not clarified, and I cannot say that the answers offered have completely resolved my uncertainties. But I have heard some convincing arguments for favoring the expansion of the teaching of religion as an independent discipline.
>
> To turn briefly to the second area, the subject matter of religion, I find it rather difficult to think of religion in general, religion with a capital "R." Religions as I have encountered them are particular: they have a certain historical and social setting. It seems to me that the manifestations of historically defined religion—the literature, history, rituals, sacraments, be-

liefs, and theologies of given religious groups—are the most appropriate objects of study in a department of religion and should form the core of courses.

Equally worthy of study are factors common to all religion, or at least to all Western religions. My own area of specialization is medieval philosophy, in which we speak of "natural theology"—the issues common to Judaism, Christianity, and Islam. As modern analogues of these studies, one might fruitfully explore what religious existentialists have in common and how the analysis of language relates to the study of religion.

I have the greatest difficulty with a third kind of subject matter: that which has to do with ancillary disciplines—the psychology of religion, the sociology of religion, and so forth—which study religion only incidentally. For example, I have some apprehension that if religious phenomena are subjected to a certain kind of psychological scrutiny, they will be relegated to the category of abnormal behavior. In a secular academic environment, this approach may be justified, but it should be properly balanced by other approaches. This is one of the reasons I want to make a firm distinction between the proper subject matter of religion and that which is ancillary.

Another sensitive area which warrants further exploration has to do with irreducible differences in the varieties of religious expression. All of us are aware that, in spite of the many common concerns that unite us, there are also obvious differences that divide us. For example, Christians and Jews share the Hebrew Bible, but they differ considerably in the way they read the document. Catholics and Protestants differ from each other in their fundamental beliefs, as do various Protestant groups. Perhaps we should have explored further how these differences may affect the college curriculum. On the simplest level: Can the average college provide a staff large enough to present adequately the variety of positions within Western religions, not to mention non-Western religions?

A fifth area of uneasiness is what I would like to call, for lack of a better term, the political factor. Legally, there seems to be no obstacle to teaching religion in colleges and universities, but what I have in mind is less tangible. How will the various religious communities react to the teaching of religion, particularly in tax-supported institutions? Some of us are concerned about how the academic study of religion may affect the religious convictions of college students. To be sure, college is quite properly the place for questioning and re-examining beliefs, but the teaching of religion touches on sensitivities that do not exist in other disciplines.

Finally, I want to comment on a point which Professor Johann articulated most fully but which I found somewhat elusive. If I understood him correctly, Professor Johann emphasized that the teacher of religion must have an involvement with his subject. If he meant by this that a good teacher should have a feeling for and interest in the subject, I find his point rather obvious and unobjectionable. But if he was saying that the teacher of religion should himself have a religious commitment, I must disagree with him. Such a commitment seems a questionable prerequisite to teaching religion under secular auspices. I acknowledge that it may be desirable if a given tradition is taught by someone who, in addition to having the proper scholarly qualifications, has some knowledge of the tradition from within, but this seems to me to be a very different point.

Professor Martin concluded the conference with a summary:

We began with an attempt to clarify the phenomena of religion. We indicated that there are some givens—institutions, beliefs, practices, people, and traditions. Then we attempted to indicate that the methodological consideration of these givens is complex because the givens themselves are complex. But their very complexity issues a kind of mandate that we not evade academic consideration of the phenomena. In our discussion, it has become obvious that when we pursue the issues involved in the question of the academic study of religion, then we find ourselves pursuing in microcosm the issues implicit in the macrocosm of liberal learning—the questions of personal involvement, of truth, of various methodological approaches. Even the problem of definition itself becomes a part of the study of religion. What I think has emerged is the notion that there are phenomena, there are givens. They exist and they require attention. They are so complex that nothing less than a family or cluster of methodologies will do if we are to attend to them properly. The recognition of their complexity and of their relevance makes it imperative that we hesitate no longer to do a better job than we are now doing.

Thus the conference ended by reaffirming the idea that universities have the responsibility of teaching religion as one highly significant aspect of human experience and that it is high time that they take cognizance of this responsibility.

APPENDIX

Participants in the
Conference on Religion as an Academic Discipline
in College and University
State University of New York at Stony Brook
January 28-29, 1966 *

Adelson, Howard L. ....Professor, Department of History, City College of New York
Belford, Lee A. ....Chairman, Department of Religious Education, New York University
Berger, Morris ....Professor, Department of Education, State University of New York at Albany
Birr, Kendall ....Chairman, Division of Social Sciences, State University of New York at Albany
Davis, I. Ridgway ....Chairman, Curricula and Courses Committee, University of Connecticut
Dougherty, The Most Rev. John J. ....President, Seton Hall University
Eddins, Berkley B. ....Professor, Department of Philosophy, State University of New York at Buffalo
Friedman, The Rev. C. W. ....Associate Secretary, College and University Department, The National Catholic Educational Association
Gant, Edward ....Provost and Vice-President, University of Connecticut
Glass, Bentley ....Academic Vice-President, Distinguished Professor of Biology, State University of New York at Stony Brook
Glasse, John ....Chairman, Department of Religion, Vassar College
Gordon, S. Stewart ....Vice-President for Academic Affairs, State University of New York at Binghamton
Gross, Mason W. ....President, Rutgers—The State University
Hakim, The Rev. Albert B. ....Dean of the College of Arts and Sciences, Seton Hall University
Hallgring, Louis ....Associate Professor, Department of History, Hunter College
Hartzell, Karl D. ....Administrative Officer, State University of New York at Stony Brook
Horowitz, Murray ....Associate Dean of the College, Brooklyn College
Hyman, Arthur ....Associate Professor of Philosophy, Yeshiva University
Johann, The Rev. Robert O., S.J. ...Professor, Department of Philosophy, Fordham University
Knight, Thomas ....Chairman, Department of Philosophy, Adelphi University
Korte, Karl ....Lecturer, Department of Music, State University of New York at Binghamton

---

* Institutional affiliations are indicated as of January 1966.

Ludlum, Robert	Dean, College of Arts and Sciences, Adelphia University
McCarron, Brother Isidore	Chairman, Department of Theology, Saint Francis College
McEwen, William P.	Dean, College of Liberal Arts and Sciences, Hofstra University
McGrade, Arthur S.	Assistant Professor, Department of Theology, University of Connecticut
McInnes, The Very Rev. William C., S.J.	President, Fairfield University
Martin, J. Alfred, Jr.	Danforth Professor of Religion in Higher Education, Union Theological Seminary
Michaelsen, Robert	Chairman, Department of Religious Studies, University of California at Santa Barbara
Mooney, The Rev. Christopher F., S.J.	Department of Theology, Fordham University
Moran, Brother C. Gabriel	Assistant Professor, Department of Theology, Manhattan College
Myers, Gerald	Chairman, Department of Philosophy, C. W. Post College
Nelson, Benjamin	Professor, Department of Sociology, State University of New York at Stony Brook
O'Dea, Thomas F.	Professor and Chairman, Department of Religion, Columbia University
Pemberton, John	Executive Director, The American Civil Liberties Union
Phenix, Philip H.	Professor of Philosophy and Education, Columbia University
Quinn, Vincent	Assistant Professor, Department of English, Brooklyn College
Reis, Lincoln	Chairman, Department of Philosophy, Long Island University
Ross, Stanley R.	Dean, College of Arts and Sciences, State University of New York at Stony Brook
Sasscer, Harrison	Program Director, Association of American Colleges
Schlatter, Richard	Provost and Vice-President, Rutgers—The State University
Seeman, Howard	Graduate Assistant, Department of Philosophy, City College of New York
Sullivan, Brother C. Stephen	Academic Vice-President, Manhattan College
Tallman, Brother Labre	Instructor, Department of Theology, Saint Francis College
Ulanov, Barry	Associate Professor, Department of English, Barnard College
Watson, Walter	Deputy Chairman, Department of Philosophy, State University of New York at Stony Brook
Wekerle, Frank	Chairman, Department of Philosophy, Hofstra University
Welch, Claude	Berg Professor and Chairman, Department of Religious Thought, University of Pennsylvania
Wilson, John F.	Assistant Professor, Department of Religion, Princeton University